GUITAR PLAYING HAWAIIAN STYLE
by Ozzie Kotani

MW00563447

Kī Hōʻalu
An Instructional
Method for
Slack Key
Volume One

Online Audio   www.melbay.com/99263MEB

Audio Contents

1	Executing A Slide [:31]	10	Ex. 4 ʻĀwīwī [1:42]
2	Executing A Pull-off [:35]	11	Ex. 5 Maunaloa [2:40]
3	Executing A Add-on [:35]	12	Ex. 6 Manamana Lele [2:29]
4	Executing A Hammer [:41]	13	The Slack G Tuning [:32]
5	Executing A Chime or Harmonic [:45]	14	Ex. 7 ʻEwalu [2:09]
6	The Taro Patch Tuning [:41]	15	Ex. 8 Kakahiaka [1:31]
7	Ex. 1 Kani Kī Hōʻalu [2:23]	16	The Drop C Tuning [:30]
8	Ex. 2 Manuela Bay [1:57]	17	Ex. 9 Namaka's Mele [:51]
9	Ex. 3 Mōlehu [2:02]		

1 2 3 4 5 6 7 8 9 0

Visit us on the Web at www.melbay.com — E-mail us at email@melbay.com

TABLE OF CONTENTS

FOREWORD

Ozzie Kotani is one of the great Hawaiian slack key guitarists. He usually plays his unique arrangements and compositions on a nylon string, "classical" guitar (he is sometimes misrepresented as a classical guitarist, which he is not). Ozzie sometimes incorporates influences outside of Hawai'i, such as Spanish, mainland American folk and popular music, Brazilian and Japanese music. He also plays great steel string guitar, often in a very different and more traditional way than his nylon string playing, and he thoroughly knows the traditions and the styles of the older slack key masters. Ozzie gets a wide variety of tones and colors out of the various tunings he uses, and he is always exploring new tunings, techniques and influences. He has great feeling and drive in his playing, and his ballads are exquisite in their soul and feeling.

Ozzie is also one of the leading educators in slack key, teaching individual students, and holding workshops. He also teaches the slack key extension course at the University of Hawai'i in Honolulu. Ozzie continually explores new ways of teaching and bringing slack key guitar to the public. This book is one of the manifestations of this endeavor.

Ozzie has recorded one album, *Classical Slack*, and we're planning on releasing several more albums of his solo material on Dancing Cat Records. His own exquisite compositions prepared especially for this book are a great way to learn the fundamentals for starting on the path of Hawaiian Slack Key Guitar. This book will be a great asset to those at any level of playing who are wanting to learn. Ozzie has worked on it for a long time with great dedication and it's great to finally have it out.

George Winston

AUTHOR'S NOTES

This book was written for all the people who love the sound of slack key guitar. Hopefully, it will reveal how the style is played whether you are a classical guitarist or a "backyard" musician without music reading skills. I felt this was the best way to share the tradition with as many people as possible, in the simplest and clearest manner, without personal instruction. Many individuals avoid classrooms, and private tutors are expensive and hard to find. This book, the first of three in the series, allows you to study at your pace with a choice of songs that appeal to your level of playing. After eleven years of teaching, I feel this book and the format Dennis and I have chosen captures my teaching method. May your enthusiasm grow as you learn this unique Hawaiian style of guitar playing!

Dedication

This book is dedicated to my late brother, Roland Motoi Kotani, whom I respected, admired, and very often sought out advice from throughout his brief but bright lifetime.

Acknowledgments

The author wishes to acknowledge the help, support, and cooperation of Dennis Ladd, a friend without whose great patience and participation this book would never have been done. I would also like to thank George "Keoki" Winston for his kindness and support over the years, for writing the introduction and for sharing so much music and information with me; Sithiporn Bob Keller for the cover; the Bishop Museum Archives for the historic photographs used in the book; Louise Kubo for trying out the book and providing invaluable notes and suggestions; Dancing Cat Productions and Windham Hill Records; Kosei Yamane for letting us photograph his Martin guitar for the cover; and Charlie Myers for the photography.

I would like to extend my sincerest gratitude to the following for their advice and encouragement on the project: Pauline Chung, Peter Medeiros, Maile Meyers and Native Books, Barbara Pope, Lance Takamiya and Marguerite Rezachek.

Ozzie Kotani

Ozzie Kotani
November, 1995

TECHNICAL NOTES

The book was done on a Macintosh Plus computer using the New Century Schoolbook font. Proof pages were printed on an Apple LaserWriter II at 300 dpi.

The tablatures were done using Aldus SuperPaint 3.0 and imported to Aldus PageMaker 4.0 for layout. All text was typed directly into PageMaker.

Photos were scanned on a Sharp XJ320 scanner at 300 dpi, 24 bit. Work on both the cover and photos was done on a Macintosh IIfx in Adobe PhotoShop 2.5. The final cover was put together using Quark Express.

Acknowledgments

Thanks first and foremost to Ozzie Kotani for calling on me to work with him on this project. What a compliment to be asked to work on something so personal and important. After more than two years of hard work, negotiating over format, and hours of writing and editing, the friendship is stronger now than it was at the beginning. Time to start volume two!

Dennis Ladd
February 1994

GUITAR PLAYING HAWAIIAN STYLE
KĪ HŌʻALU

Slack-key guitar playing is found only in Hawaiʻi. The rhythms and movement of the music, the picking styles and embellishments make the sound of slack-key guitar distinct to the listener. Certain strings in the tunings used are often lowered ("slacked") from the classical or standard tuning—thus the name, *slack-key*. The Hawaiian name for the style is *kī hōʻalu*, kī being the Hawaiianization of "key" and hōʻalu meaning "to slacken or loosen." A main feature of the style is that the player picks an alternating bass pattern with the thumb while playing a melody with the fingers. Originally developed as an accompaniment to the voice, the music reflects traditional hula rhythms and vocal techniques used in chanting and singing.

THE HISTORY OF SLACK-KEY

Any history of slack key is largely theoretical because there is very little documentation recording the development of the style through the years. With Honolulu being a center of trade and provisioning during the early 1800s, it is very possible that the guitar was introduced during this period by Mexicans and Californians. Considerable trading took place between Valparaiso (Mexico) and Lahaina between 1800 and 1820.

One cannot exclude the possibility that the guitar was in the Islands at an even earlier date considering the popularity of the instrument in New England, home for many of the whalers and missionaries who came to Hawaiʻi, and the frequency of ships from the northeastern coast of America in the Pacific.

The theory given most often, however, credits the *vaqueros* or cowboys of Southern California who arrived to control a wild cattle problem in the Big Island in 1832. Along with riding and roping skills, they brought their guitars. We can only assume that they taught the Hawaiian cowboys or *paniolos*, or more likely that the paniolos taught themselves, how to play the instrument over a period of time.

The fact that the style is unique reflects the creativity of the Hawaiians and their musical awareness. Perhaps the vaqueros were in the Islands for too short a time for a Spanish influence to take hold in the music. It seems more likely that the Hawaiians chose to tune the guitar to suit their tastes—perhaps to fit their vocal range, perhaps to accompany the voice with a more suitable or familiar rhythmic pattern. The only pre-Western Hawaiian instruments were percussive, with the exception of the *ʻūkēkē* which is similar to the Jew's harp. It is not surprising that slack-key music is characterized by a repetitive rhythm reflecting the chant and hula tradition.

A major period of development for slack-key occurred during the reign of King David Kalākaua who was responsible for the cultural resurgence of the 1880s and 1890s. His coronation in 1883 and jubilee in 1886 included performances of chant and hula during a period when missionaries viewed such activities as "pagan." His conviction that the revitalization of culture in the people formed the roots to the support and survival of the Hawaiian kingdom remains a major factor in the continuing practice of traditional music and dance today. While he supported the preservation of ancient music, he also encouraged the addition of introduced instruments such as the ʻukulele and guitar.

In fact, it was at Kalākaua's coronation that the guitar was featured in combination with the *ipu* (gourd drum) and *pahu* (hula drum) in a form called *hula ku'i*. This mixing of the old and new led to the popularity of the guitar as well as the 'ukulele.

Today, slack-key guitar is widely enjoyed and its sound is reaching out beyond the islands. Styles of playing have developed and virtuosos have created pieces which bring out the beauty and diversity of slack-key guitar not only as an accompaniment to singing but as a solo instrumental form as well.

TUNINGS

The number of tunings used in slack key is not known because the possibilities are nearly limitless. Estimates have ranged from thirty-nine that have been recorded (including standard tuning). Few guitarists play—not *know of*, mind you, but *play*— beyond ten tunings, if that many. Most of the slack-key artists today favor a few tunings of choice based upon a certain sound characteristic to these tunings. The fingering involved and the tradition followed are also factors.

In earlier times, tunings were not shared and were meant to be kept within the *'ohana* or extended family much like the genealogical chants. Certain tuning and playing styles were associated with different families. Tunings were sometimes named after a player. An example of this is Namakelua's tuning, also called *Wahine* tuning (DGDF#BD).

There are two terms of note used in the past to differentiate between tunings. *Kī ho'oku'u* referred to *open* tunings in which a chord could be played without having to hold or fret any of the strings. Tunings such as *Taro Patch* (DGDGBD) and *Open D* (DADF#AD) would fall into this category. *Kī pa'a* or *ho'opa'a* referred to tunings in which a string or strings had to be held or fretted to make a chord. Tunings like *Maunaloa* (CGEGAE) or *Slack G* (DGDF#BD) would characterize this type.

Secrecy is a thing of the past and tunings have been openly shared and documented by such notables as Leonard Kwan, Gabby Pahinui, Raymond Kane and Keola Beamer (who came out with the first instructional book on slack-key guitar). Slack-key masters Sonny Chillingworth and Raymond Kane have offered private lessons to a new generation of players who will ensure the perpetuation of their tunings and styles.

Although an unknown number of tunings exist, it is not true that a good slack-key player is one who knows numerous tunings. More so, it is the guitarist's ability to bring out the beauty and uniqueness of slack-key in a tuning which stands as a measure of advancement and maturity in the tradition.

ORNAMENTATIONS

The proficiency with which a slack-key guitarist uses various ornamentations in an original and creative manner—in combination with a playing or picking style— marks his or her individuality or identity. These ornamentations include slides, pull-offs, hammering (which reflect a favored vocal technique used in chant and song), harmonics (also referred to as *bells* or *chimes* and which may be an attempt to mimic falsetto style singing), vibrato (which creates *chicken skin* slack-key), damping of the strings, strumming between picking, picking close to the bridge (to get a more brilliant sound), and percussive techniques such as striking the guitar body or slapping the strings.

Slack-key comes from an oral tradition and the earlier players all learned by watching and listening to experienced guitarists. The music was never taught in a notated form and the skills needed by a student were a good ear, a good memory, and a good sense of timing. This is the reason for the diversity of styles and the development of virtuosos. Few restrictions applied, unlike classical guitar, and after completing a period of instruction and practice, a player was free to experiment within a certain framework of chords and rhythms. The great slack-key artists whose playing techniques and style are original and identifiable include Philip "Gabby" Pahinui, Leland "Atta" Isaacs, the late Sonny Chillingworth, Leonard Kwan, Raymond Kane, Fred Punahoa, Peter Moon, Ledward Ka'apana, Keola Beamer, and Cyril Pahinui.

IMPROVISATION

An important aspect of slack-key guitar is improvisation. Variations of the melody are common and the player often dictates the movement of a piece according to his or her personal interpretation. Jam sessions involving a group of guitarists provide an opportunity to improvise solos during their breaks. Playing counter melody and exposure to new techniques as well as learning how to accompany are important skills developed from these experiences with other musicians. Such encounters nurture creativity and spontaneity in slack-key guitar playing.

Improvisation comes with maturity as a player. As you begin to familiarize yourself with a tuning, such things as chord positions and variations, where and how runs can occur, and fingering techniques and picking patterns begin to open up possibilities of improvisation. This, in combination with what is referred to as the *feeling* for the music, creates the sound of slack-key. Flamenco guitar has its counterpart in the term *el duende* or the *spirit* of the playing.

Slack-key professionals will often play a piece repeatedly and not do it the same way twice. The use of various kinds of audio equipment gives today's student of slack-key guitar other alternatives for learning skills vital to improvisation.

VARIATIONS OF GUITAR PLAYING

There are several variations of guitar playing in Hawai'i that have been used in the past and are worth mentioning:

1. "Needle and Thread" was a technique which employed the use of a large sewing needle attached to a length of thread or string. The thread was held in the mouth while the needle rested lightly over the strings of the slightly tilted guitar in the area of the sound hole. When the strings of the guitar were plucked, the needle vibrated against the strings producing a unique sound.

2. An interesting variation was used by a suitor to serenade his sweetheart. A string was connected in some manner from the guitar body to the window of the guitarist's loved one. While playing, the string was pulled taut and used to transmit the sound to the window which acted as a resonator.

3. *Hoʻopāpā* or *pāpā* were the words used to describe the playing of harmonics, also called *chimes* or *bells* in slack-key guitar. Natural harmonics occurring on the fifth, seventh, and the twelfth frets are most commonly used. This technique is used to great advantage in the popular tune, "Maui Chimes."

CLOSING NOTES

There have been several reasons given for the lack of interest nationally and internationally in slack-key guitar. The style has often been called simple in terms of chordal structure and limited in terms of technical features. The music has been termed too "local" to stimulate much appeal to a wider, far-ranging audience. It has been said that slack-key music has not been notated, with some exceptions, due to the fact that it posed no challenge to people capable of notation. These statements were commonly heard in the 1970s.

Slack-key is experiencing a resurgence in popularity today propelled by musicians like Gabby Pahinui who brought new life to the style by expanding upon techniques and arrangements, and Raymond Kane who was the recipient of the National Heritage Fellowship Award in 1987. Pianist and guitarist George Winston has been a major force in the promotion and exposure of slack-key at a national level and is in the process of releasing recordings by some of the great artists who have influenced the younger generation of players.

Courses are being offered at many community centers and colleges utilizing the tablature notation method. Annual concerts feature guest players from Japan and San Francisco. In summary, slack-key is far from dying out and is here to stay. Steps are being taken to ensure the continuation of the tradition. Its elements of uniqueness should never be ignored and hopefully there will be a greater appreciation in the future.

SOURCES

Beamer, Keola. *Keola Beamer's First Method for Hawaiian Slack-Key Guitar.*

Buck, Peter H. *Arts and Crafts of Hawaii. Vol. 9. Musical Instruments.*

The Hawaiian Music Foundation. *Haʻilono Mele.* Vol. I, No. 1: 4, 6; Vol. I, No. 2: 2; Vol. I, No. 4: 4; Vol. I, No. 6: 2; Vol. I, No. 12: 1; Vol. III, No. 5: 4—7.

Kahananui, Dorothy M. *Music of Ancient Hawaii, a Brief Survey*: 12—15.

Malm, William P. *Music Cultures of the Pacific, the Near East, and Asia*: 14—16.

Tatar, Elizabeth. "Slack Key Guitar." *Hawaiian Music and Musicians, An Illustrated History edited by George S. Kanahele* : 350—360.

Tava, Reri. *Raymond Kane, Hawaiian Slack Key Guitar.*

Todaro, Tony. *Tony Todaro Presents: The Golden Years of Hawaiian Entertainment. 1874—1974.*

Liner Notes for "The Old Way—Slack Key by Leonard Kwan." Tradewinds Records.

HOW TO READ THE TABLATURE

Understanding this section is absolutely essential to making this book work. To make it easier for yourself, remember this:

1). Don't be intimidated by the lines and numbers that you see.
2). You don't need the ability to read music or have any prior musical training or background.
3). Many of the slack key players don't read music, including the author of this book.

One of the goals in doing this book was to remove or keep to a minimum much of the musical notation used in other books.

What you see in tablature notation is six lines which represent the six strings of the guitar. The important thing to remember is that the top line represents the first or highest pitched string while the bottom line represents the sixth or lowest pitched string. In other words, it is an illustration of a guitar turned upside down. This probably causes the most confusion for the beginning readers but once becoming oriented they have few problems.

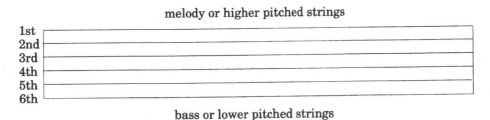

On these lines will be numbers which correspond to the frets on the guitar neck. Each number represents a note to be played. At the same time, they also indicate which of the strings should be plucked. For example, a "0" on the 5th string means that the string is to be left open or unfretted while being played, while a "5" on the top or first string tells the player that the string is held down on the 5th fret while being plucked:

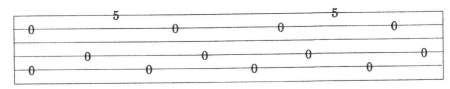

Tablature is read from left to right and gives the sequence or order of the strings being played. Tablatures in this book are divided into segments by a vertical line. These segments are called measures. Every 5th measure is marked:

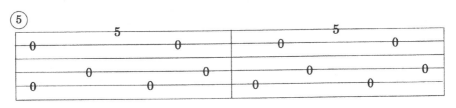

Numbers written vertically are to be played at the same time by "pinching" or "brushing." In a nutshell, tablature shows the players where to hold with the left hand and what to pluck with the right. The major element often missing from tablature notation is the time value. Here, brackets at the bottom of the tablature mark the main beats of the music (played by the thumb) and brackets on the top mark off-beats (usually fingered).

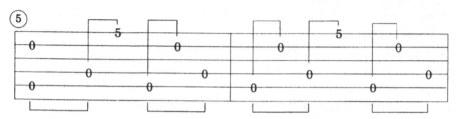

A Compact Disc of all the songs is provided so you can hear the rhythm and timing of each piece as well as the tuning. Hopefully, the music and the tabs will work together and make learning slack key easier.

A NOTE ON READING TABLATURE

Before leaving this section, emphasis should be made on two points:

First, **don't give a spatial value to the numbers on the lines**. In other words, don't judge timing based on how close or far apart the numbers are. This is a common error—listen to the accompanying CD for correct timing.

Second, tablatures best serve as references after learning a piece. **Don't become dependent on the tablatures to play a song. Memorize the piece and get away from the tablatures as soon as possible.** You can then play or perform without the hindrance of paper, music stands, etc. You will also find that you can then put more attention into improving techniques and the overall sound of each song.

THE RIGHT HAND TECHNIQUE

The choice of fingers used to pluck the strings and the style of picking varies among slack-key players. There are several factors that explain this: a desire to emulate a player or teacher or to carry on the tradition in a manner of playing; the tuning that the player learns and plays in; the eventual repertoire and style that a player expands into; the use of finger picks or even the guitar itself—all contribute towards a favored technique.

Regardless of the style you eventually settle into, the thumb picks the alternating bass while a finger or fingers pluck a melody line on the higher pitched strings. Whether using a two, three or four-finger picking style, you should strive for a clean and clear sound which can be maintained regardless of the tempo or volume of your playing. It is important that the right hand be relaxed and in a comfortable position for the player.

THE LEFT HAND TECHNIQUE

The development of the left hand is directly related to the amount of practice the player puts in. Finger dexterity and strength are necessities in the playing of slack-key. As you learn the positions, chords, and techniques, practice becomes the key element in "cleaning up" the sound. Positioning of the wrist enables the player to hold down the desired strings cleanly without contacting other strings. Holding down the strings between the frets rather than on the frets ensures clearer notes. Placement of the thumb on the back of the guitar neck provides the needed reinforcement to hold down the guitar strings with sufficient pressure. Failure to do so results in buzzing and muffled sounds. Finally, the position of the elbow and its proximity to the left side of the player's body provides the angle needed to clear certain chords and fingerings on the guitar neck.

POSITIONING THE GUITAR

The main point is to be comfortable. Whether you choose to play using a footstand in a classical position or with legs crossed and the guitar tilted, you should feel relaxed and unstrained. The position should not hinder movement of either arm or cut off circulation from your arm or leg. One thing to remember when learning slack-key is that the style comes from an oral or unwritten tradition. No position or manner of playing is standardized or recognized as the "correct" way. Of course, positioning is important in achieving a good attack on the strings but it should be the choice of the individual. It is not a discipline of the style.

OPEN AND CLOSED POSITIONS

One of the key concepts in the playing of slack-key melodies is that of open and closed positions. In the Taro Patch Tuning, these positions are played specifically on the third and first strings. These positions are based on chords and chord names are identified with them. Open positions on the third and first strings have a single fret between them; closed positions are held on adjacent frets, with no fret dividing them.

It is important for you to use the pointer or index finger on the third string. The first string can be held by either the ring or little finger. The author uses the little finger which allows for a longer reach and also frees the ring and middle fingers to move on higher strings or complete chord structures in more technical pieces. Most of the other slack-key players past and present appear to favor the ring finger on the first string. Whatever your choice may be, you should stay with the combination in doing both open and closed positions. Use the inlays in the neck of the guitar for guides in finding frets. Usually, a guitar will have inlays marking the third, fifth, seventh, ninth, twelfth and fourteenth frets on the neck. If there are no markings, it is suggested that you use tape or whiteout as temporary indicators of these key frets.

Exercise 3, "Mōlehu," will expose you to these positions. In any measure, whenever the third and first strings have a "4" and "5," a "7" and "9," or any combination as shown on the diagram, these more than likely reflect closed and open positions—with the possible addition of another string. For example, the introduction sequence in the exercise is a series of open and closed positions with the addition of the bass line. The pointer and ring or little finger combination should move along the third and first strings together.

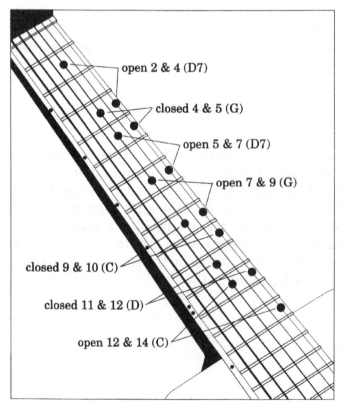

open 2 & 4 (D7)

closed 4 & 5 (G)

open 5 & 7 (D7)

open 7 & 9 (G)

closed 9 & 10 (C)

closed 11 & 12 (D)

open 12 & 14 (C)

THE ALTERNATING BASS

One of the major challenges in the playing of traditional or solo slack-key is the alternating bass. It is a feature that characterizes the style and gives it the full sound which needs no accompaniment. Timing and finger coordination play vital roles.

The meter of a piece is set through the bass line. Excluding advanced or contemporary slack-key arrangements, failure to keep an even tempo or rhythm on the bass strings results in choppy or disjointed playing. Alternating bass should be learned in a progressive manner. Exercises, such as the first one in this book, having a slow or moderate tempo and a bass pattern that falls on the downbeat, should serve well as starters for the beginning player. This is the time to get the fundamentals of the style down. This is the time to get it right! Sloppy playing with missing or wrong bass lines and habits which are hard to break will be the end result if you don't. As you get accustomed to the alternating bass, move at your own pace. Don't rush it.

Finger coordination is also needed because while the thumb plays a bass pattern, other fingers will carry the melodic line. As with learning alternating bass, slow and simple are best at first. Melodies using few strings and having repeated moves are best for the beginner. Be aware that the choice of fingers used to pick the higher strings should be considered.

The bass line will commonly be played on the sixth, fifth, and fourth strings—the top three—and often reflects hula rhythms. There are tunings, however, such as the "Maunaloa Tuning" which will have a bass occurring all the way down to the third string.

EXECUTING TECHNIQUES AND ORNAMENTATIONS

The following is an explanation of the mechanics involved in playing various special embellishments commonly used in slack-key guitar playing. Examples from the book will appear with the explanations so you can see how we have notated each technique.

Slides

Slides are played by holding down a string on a given fret, plucking the string, then sliding your finger to another fret with a constant pressure applied through the movement. Be careful that the slide moves fully from one fret to the other. A constant, even pressure during the slide will ensure a clean and defined sound. Sliding can be done on any string and can move up or down the guitar neck. The movement can be from one fret to the adjacent fret or it can range over several frets. Slides, by tradition, are most often used on single strings although slides using more than one string (1st and 3rd for example) are becoming more common. Raymond Kane is one of the great slack-key artists who uses the sliding technique to its fullest.

Sliding

1. Hold down the given string on the given fret (in this case, fret 4).
2. Pluck the string.
3. Slide the finger, while pressing the string down, to the next given fret (5).
4. Slides are notated with a curved line linking two numbers.

Pull-Offs

Pull-offs involve holding down a string on a given fret, plucking the string, then pulling down with the finger holding the string as you release it. This creates a unique plucked second note from the left hand. Pull down strongly in a controlled manner to get the percussive, striking sound desired rather than a weak, soft sound. Pull-offs are used mainly on the open melody strings but are also used while holding a string and pulling off on a higher fret, often while holding a chord position. Innovative slack-key virtuoso Peter Moon displays clean and solid technique in doing series of pull-offs in his recordings.

Pulling-Off

1. Hold down the given string on the given fret (in this case, fret 2).
2. Pluck the string.
3. Pull down with the finger holding the string while you release it (0).
4. Pull-offs are notated with a curved line linking two numbers, with the letters "po" as shown.

Add-Ons

By plucking a string and then bringing your finger down on the string at a given fret (without plucking the string again), you can play a second, softened sound. The sound of this slurred, unplucked movement is best described as a "ta-la" sound in contrast to a plucked "ta-ta" sound. The string has to be initially plucked strongly enough and your finger has to come down hard enough on the desired fret to make this technique work effectively. Like most of the ornamentations discussed, this one can also be used on any string.

Adding-On

1. Leave the given string open (in this case, the 1st string).
2. Pluck the string.
3. Bring a finger down on the string at the given fret (2nd) without plucking the string again.
4. Add-ons are notated with a curved line linking a "0" to a second number, as shown.

Hammers

This ornamentation, which reflects a favored vocal technique used in chanting and singing, is basically the combination of adding-on and pulling-off in rapid succession. Pluck the string, bring your finger down at a given fret and pull it quickly off again, either by pulling down or "kicking" up on the string without plucking it again. You want a strong, even motion with the percussive sound that characterizes this technique.

Pulling down while releasing is probably the easier and more common movement used by slack-key guitarists today. Raymond Kane is one of the few who gets a clean hammering sound by "kicking" up on the string. This technique is harder in that there is a tendency to strike the string above the one being hammered but the point is made that the finger ends up in a better position to come back down on a string. Hammering is used commonly on the open first string but often is played from a chord position or on other strings. Slack-key master Sonny Chillingworth uses hammering to create some of his signature "vamps" and picking sequences.

Hammers

1. Leave the given string open (in this case, the 1st string).
2. Pluck the string.
3. Bring a finger down on the string at the given fret (2nd) without plucking the string.
4. Pull down (or kick up) while releasing—again without plucking the string.
5. Hammers are notated with a curved line linking three numbers, as shown.

Chimes or Harmonics

Sometimes referred to as "bells," this technique works on position and touch. A finger is placed very lightly on a string over the 5th, 7th or 12th fret bar. These are the positions where natural harmonics occur and are used in slack-key guitar. Place your finger directly over the fret bar with almost no pressure. Too much pressure or not having your finger directly over the fret bar will not produce a clear tone. Clear harmonics are also harder to achieve on nylon strings and do not ring out as long as on steel strings. The age and quality of the strings or the quality of the guitar can also pose problems for the beginner. Finally, the picking of the right hand needs to be strong enough the carry the sound of the harmonic. The author uses the top section of the middle finger of the left hand to play harmonics while other players utilize the ring or little finger. For more information see "Variations of Guitar Playing" on page 3 in this book.

Chiming

1. Place the finger of your left hand **very** lightly on the string over the fret bar.
2. Pluck the string with your right hand.
3. Raise the finger of your left hand from the string to allow the string to ring.
4. Chimes are notated with an asterisk above the number, as shown.

CLOSING NOTES

Ornamentations involve movements that need to be practiced repeatedly and experimented with in order to decide which finger or fingers best facilitate the move for you. Start slowly, get comfortable with a technique and then utilize it in the context of a particular piece. In doing so, you will begin to see how the use of certain fingers are preferable over others in moving to other frets or chord positions while you are playing. It is important that the timing or meter is not affected by any added movement and keep in mind that ornamentations are exactly that—they embellish or add to a piece. You determine what you enjoy hearing and feel comfortable doing. Fancier is not always better if you lose the clarity of your playing or the steadiness of the meter. Proficient slack-key players use a mixture of techniques in creative and innovative ways that often make their playing identifiable and unique. Ornamentations vary according to the tunings used and each tuning has its limitations. The explanation of slurs, vibrato, the use of dynamics and other techniques featured in the playing of advanced slack-key will be covered in detail in another book.

MUSICAL TERMS AND NOTATIONS

Besides the tablature notations, a few musical terms and notations are used in this book:

ritard.: from the Italian word *ritardando* meaning to "slow down." You will find this noted at the end of many of the pieces in this book. The purpose of slowing down is for dramatic effect and, though you may find yourself excited at reaching the conclusion of an exercise, discipline yourself to control the tempo or speed of your playing. By doing so, you will not only pull your listeners in for the final stroke of the piece but, more importantly, you will have started giving a sense of movement to the music.

sustain: indicates that a note should be held and allowed to ring out for a second or so. This is done by making sure that the last string plucked is held down with constant pressure by the finger. Sustains are often played before going out or ending a piece and often is noted at the end of a section marked "rit."

repeat: two dots to the **left** of a bar indicates you should go back and repeat a section marked by the last two dots to the **right** of a bar. For example, in exercise 1 ("Kani Kī Hōʻalu"), you will encounter repeat signs at the end of measure 5 which tells you to go back to measure 1 where you see two dots to the right of the bar. Playing through measures 1 through 5 again, you now proceed into measure 6 and continue on until you encounter repeat signs at the end of measure 10. You now repeat back to the measure 6 (not 1) where the last two dots to the right of the bar is seen. Repeat signs are used to cut down the length of tablature notation and the reason for repeating is to restate a section and to lengthen the piece.

An important note on repeats: Notation such as "ritard." (to slow down) are to be used only on the second or repeated section.

coda: represented by a cross within a circle, a coda sign indicates a leap over several measures to a second coda sign. This often occurs in pieces where a section, oftentimes the starting section, is repeated *up to a certain measure* before going into the ending sequence. It is a good idea to look over a tablature to see if and where codas and other notations are marked.

vamp: a short musical interlude that separates verses or sections of music. There are traditional vamps shared by most players and others that are unique to individual players.

Each exercise in this book will include playing hints which will point out suggested fingerings, chords being held and any notations not discussed above.

BEFORE WE BEGIN

Before starting any exercise, it is suggested that you do the following:

1. Read the introduction to the piece and the hints for playing the exercise.
2. Look over the tablature for repeated sections and the use of codas. Review any notations that are new to you.
3. Listen to the CD to get an idea of how the piece sounds.
4. Listen to the song again. This time, try and follow along with the tablature.
5. Pick up your guitar and get into the correct tuning by using the CD, by fretting the strings, or by using an electronic tuner.
6. Begin the exercise.

It is very important to remember that you do not have to play as fast as the recording!

As a rule of thumb, you should always start by playing slowly in learning a piece. Work towards setting a nice and even tempo with your bass line. Determine which fingers work best for the movements required to play the melody. Experiment using different fingers to play with. You may like the way it sounds slow. If not, you can always play faster after you are comfortable with the exercise.

HOW TO USE THE INSTRUCTIONAL CD

After you have listened at least twice to the exercise you'll be working on, place the recording at the beginning of the piece. Listen to just a measure or two of the exercise, then stop the recording. Try to play what you have just heard. If you can't quite get it, repeat the procedure. If you feel you've probably got it, go to the next measure or so. You should always go back and play your guitar from the beginning of the tablature, or at least the measures leading up to where you left off, to get a sense of how the music flows from measure to measure. In this way you will progressively work an exercise to its conclusion or completion.

Another suggestion is that you try and play along with the recording. This will help you to identify any problems you may be having with the timing or tempo of the exercise.

HOW TO USE THE HINTS SECTIONS

After the tablature for each piece there are several pages of hints. Measures are printed along with the explanation. The parts being explained are darker than the rest. If chord positions are held, there is also a chord chart below each chord. As an example, here is the diagram from the first two measures of exercise 3, "Mōlehu":

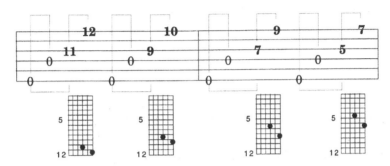

As you can see, the open and closed positions are in bold, darker print and the chord diagrams are under each new position. The chord diagrams represent the neck of the guitar with the 1st or highest string on the right. This matches the top line of tablature. The fifth and 12th frets have been marked on the diagrams. This will help you visualize the positions your left hand will hold.

The text will explain the fingering that the author uses. Sometimes you will be offered an alternative fingering. As a convention, the author calls the fingers the pointer finger, middle finger, ring finger and little finger as in the diagram below:

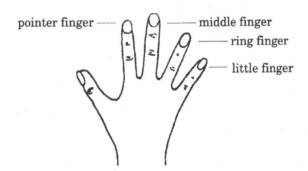

Think of the hints section as a teacher's voice that is always there to help you over the rough spots.

CHOOSING A PICKING STYLE

While the thumb plays the alternating bass line on the top three strings of the guitar, you now have to choose fingers to play the melody on the first, second, and third strings:

1. You can have your pointer or index finger play all three strings using a two finger (thumb and pointer) picking style. This is a style used on certain songs by some of the older players like Raymond Kane and Sonny Chillingworth.

2. A three finger picking style involves the thumb playing bass while the pointer picks the third string, the middle finger or pointer picks the second string, and the middle finger the first string. This seems to be the combination many players have favored.

3. The author uses a four finger method with the thumb on the bass strings, the pointer on the third string, middle finger on the second string, and ring finger on the first string. Although not commonly used in the tradition, this style is favored for an easier transition to and from classical and folk guitar playing.

Keep in mind that there is no "correct" way to play slack key guitar. You should do what works for you. This means that much of what you read in this book regarding fingering or picking are suggestions from the author. It is very true that in slack key guitar playing, no picking style can be called better than another. There are great players in every style. The three descriptions given above are general and there is no strict or rigid "assignment" of fingers. There are players who use their thumb on the melody strings at times, or switch from two or three finger style based upon the tuning or piece. There are even a few players who use a five finger technique. Stay free from any western music concepts of discipline.

STANDARDIZE FINGERING AND PICKING

While there is no restriction in the choosing of a picking style, once the choice is made, *stick to it*. Although you may decide to make a change as you progress through the book, try to keep a consistency in your playing. In other words, if you find it comfortable to pick the first string with your middle finger in measure one of the exercise, try to always pick that string with your middle finger throughout the piece.

This also applies to the fingering on the guitar neck. You should experiment with techniques and ornamentations to find what fingers work best for you. At some point in time, however, standardize your fingering. Decide what finger you like to chime or hammer with and set it!

TARO PATCH TUNING
D G D G B D

The Taro Patch Tuning is the one many slack-key guitarists first learn to play in. Also known as the Open G Tuning, it is versatile and a good one to practice basic skills such as the alternating bass and ornamentations including hammering and chiming.

From the standard "EADGBE" tuning, the sixth string or top bass string is lowered from E to D. This D note can be found on a standard pitch pipe; on the piano as the D below middle C; or as the lower octave to the fourth string which is already tuned to a D. Next, by holding down the fifth fret of the tuned sixth string you will get a G which is the note the fifth string will be lowered to. After lowering the A to a G, the fifth string can be held on the seventh fret to check the D on the fourth string. Now, hold the fourth string on the fifth fret to check the G on the third string. The third string held on the fourth fret will give you the B for the second string. Finally, the second string held on the third fret will give you a D to which the first string will be lowered.

Therefore, EADGBE becomes DGDGBD and, when strummed, will make a G chord. "Open G" refers to this aspect of the tuning by which a chord is formed with the "open" or unfretted strings. A good way to check or fine tune the guitar is to listen to the sixth, fourth and first strings which are all D notes and to the G notes on the fifth and third strings.

Some students have opted for the use of an electronic tuner which indicates when a string is in tune to a particular note. Tuning devices such as pitch pipes, tuning forks, and electronic tuners are available in most musical equipment stores.

To simplify and shorten tuning procedures, the following method will be used for the rest of the book. The first line will indicate the strings of the guitar:

6 5 4 3 2 1

The second line will indicate what fret the string should be held to get the note for the following open string:

6 5 4 3 2 1
5 7 5 4 3

Therefore, the sixth string held on the fifth fret will give the note for the fifth string, the fifth string held on the seventh fret will give the note for the fourth string, and so forth.

Exercise 1
Kani Kī Hōʻalu
Taro Patch—DGDGBD

"Kani Kī Hōʻalu" means "slack key sound" in Hawaiian.

Photo: Three female dancers with guitarist, pre-1900. Courtesy of Bishop Museum Archives.

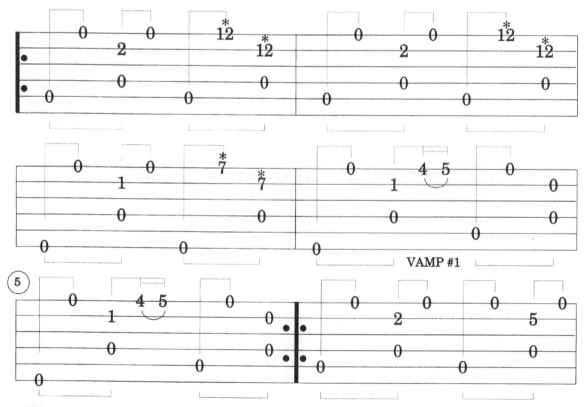

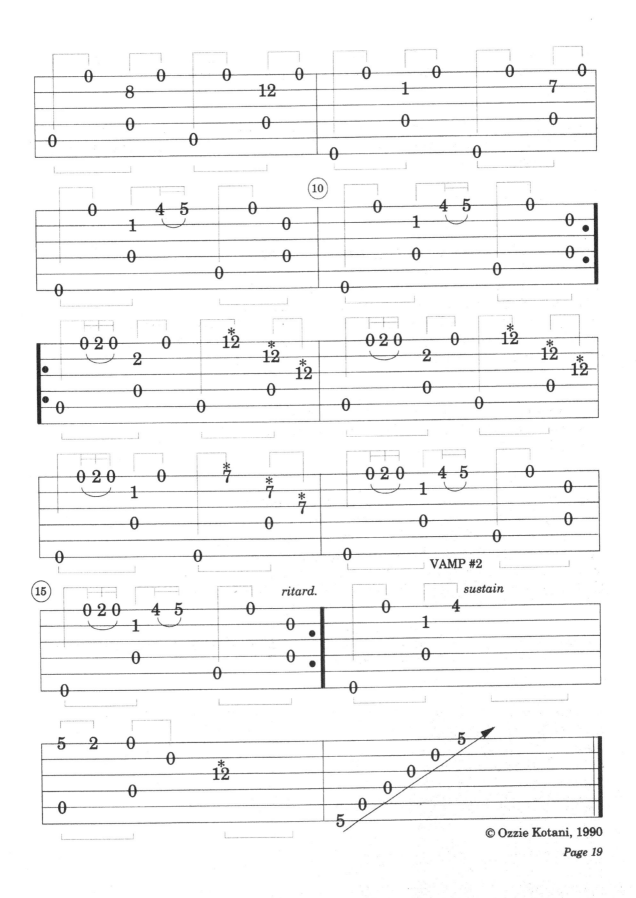

The author uses the following fingers in this exercise: the pointer finger holds the second string on the first fret only; the middle finger holds down all other frets on the second string.

In measures 4 and 14, you will see that two of the vamps have been labelled to help you recognize how vamps are used. Each is slightly different. You can review the paragraph about vamps on page 13.

Each section is played twice.

measure 1: Use your middle finger on the 2nd string, 2nd fret and for both chimes on the 1st and 2nd strings at the 12 fret. Look at the section about chiming on page 11. If it is very difficult for you to get harmonics or chimes in

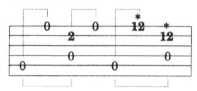

the exercise, you can hold the strings on the given fret. Use one finger, your pointer or middle, to hold both strings. Don't give up working on your chimes, though: clear, ringing chimes are a part of the classic slack key sound.

measure 3: Use your pointer finger on the 2nd string, 1st fret and your middle finger for the chimes on the 1st and 2nd strings, 7th fret.

measure 4: Use your pointer finger on the 2nd string, 1st fret. The author uses his little finger to slide from the 4th fret into the 5th fret on the 1st string. The other option would be the ring finger. This minimizes hand movement on the neck of the guitar. You will recognize

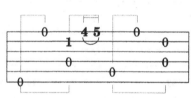

this as a much-used vamp at the end of verses in slack key music.

measure 5: The repeat sign tells you to go back to measure 1 and play the entire 5 measures again before going on to measure 6.

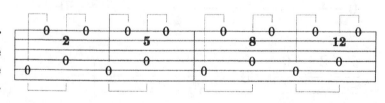

measure 6—7: Use your middle finger to climb the neck of the guitar. Release each note quickly after playing it.

measure 10: The repeat sign sends you back to measure 6 to play this section again. Then go on to measure 11.

measure 11: Play the hammer with the middle finger on the 1st string (see page 10 for the section about hammers). The same finger then holds the second string on the 2nd fret. An option is to hammer with the ring finger and follow with the middle finger on the second string.

Do not let the fretted second string ring out too long. Release the fret being held as soon as you pluck the next string.

measure 13: Played the same as measure 11, except that you use your pointer on the 2nd string, 1st fret.

measure 15: The repeat sign again sends you back to measure 11 to start the section over a second time.

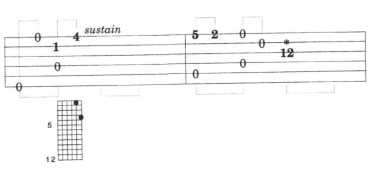

measures 16—17: Hold the chord position in measure 16, pausing before going on to measure 17. Measure 17 is played slowly and deliberately. Use your little finger on the 1st string, 5th fret and your pointer on the 1st string, 2nd fret. To play the chime on the 3rd string, 12th fret, use your middle finger.

measure 18: The last measure is a slowly strummed chord. The author holds the 6th string, 5th fret with his thumb, the 1st string, 5th fret with his ring finger. You can also use your middle finger on the 6th string, 5th fret and your ring finger on the 1st string, 5th fret.

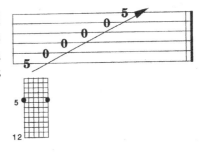

Exercise 2
Manuela Boy
Taro Patch—DGDGBD

"Manuela Boy" is an old and popular folk song with many variations in the verses.

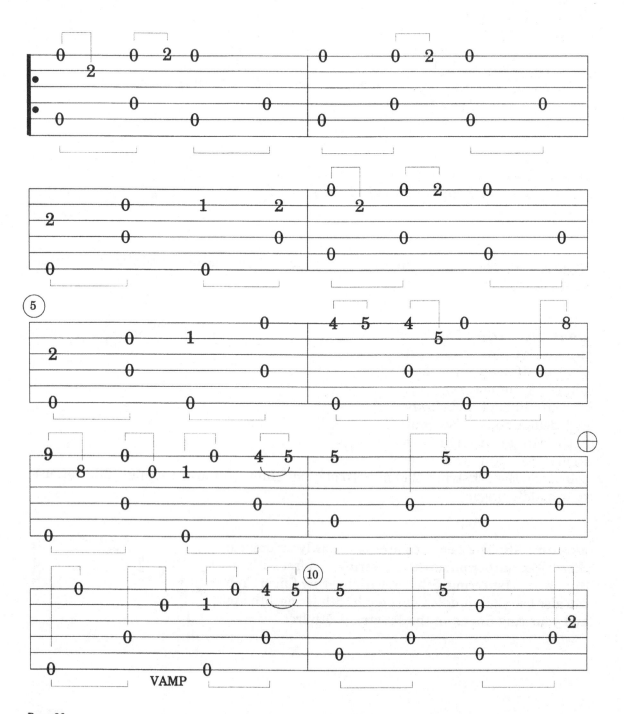

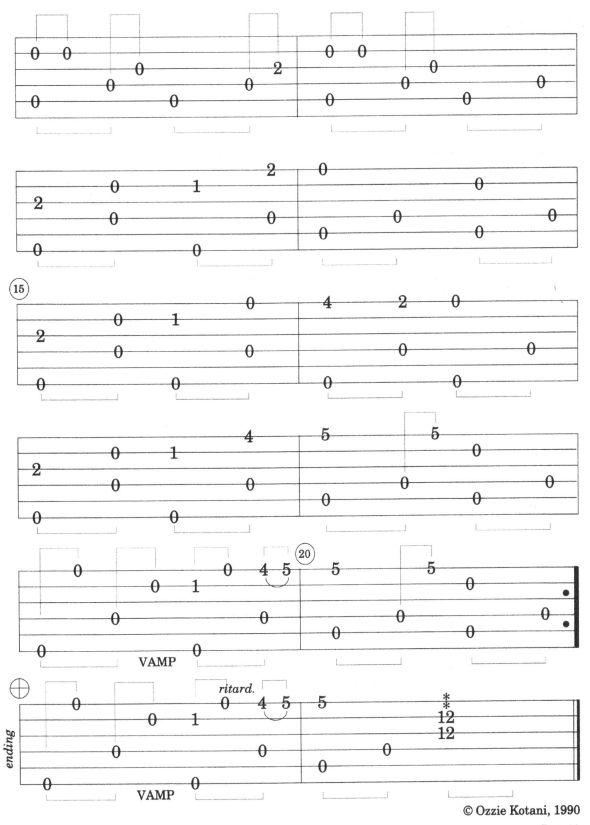

measures 1—2: Use your middle finger on both the 1st and 2nd strings, 2nd fret. This will be true for most of the tune.

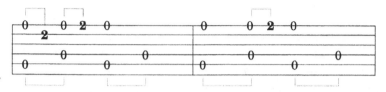

measure 3: Use your middle finger on the 3rd string, 2nd fret; your pointer finger on the 2nd string, 1st fret; and your middle finger on the 2nd string, 2nd fret.

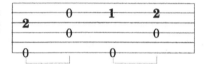

measure 6: Use your pointer finger on the 1st string, 4th fret; then add your middle finger on the 1st string, 5th fret. Leave your pointer on the 1st string and move your middle finger to the 2nd string, 5th fret.

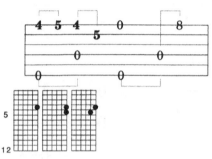

measures 6—7: Use your pointer finger on the 1st string, 8th fret; then add your middle finger on the 1st string, 9th fret. Move your pointer to the 2nd string, 8th fret.

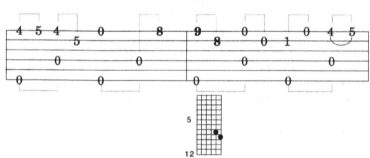

measure 7, 9, 19 and 21: Use your pointer finger to play the 2nd string, 1st fret. The author then uses his little finger to slide from the 4th fret to the 5th fret on the 1st string. The other option suggested would be the ring finger. This is to minimize hand movement on the neck of the guitar.

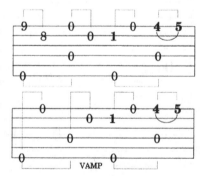

measure 16: Use your ring finger on the 1st string, 4th fret and your pointer finger on the 1st string, 2nd fret.

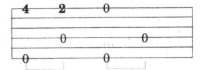

measure 17: In this sequence, you will build the position slowly. Use your middle finger on the 3rd string, 2nd fret. Then add your pointer finger on the 2nd string, 1st fret and your little finger on the 1st string, 4th fret. This is a stretch for your fingers but keep working on it until it is comfortable.

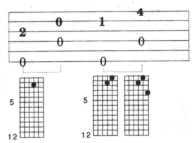

measure 20: The repeat sign sends you back to measure one to begin the piece again. Play through measure 8 where you see the coda (⊕) sign. Skip from there to the second coda sign at measure 21 to finish.

measure 22: Look at page 11 to review playing chimes. The author uses his middle finger to play both notes on the 2nd and 3rd strings above the 12th fret.

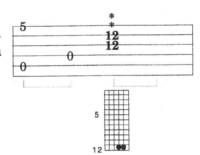

Exercise 3
Mōlehu
Taro Patch—DGDGBD

"Mōlehu" means "twilight" or "dusk." The piece should be played slowly and *nahenahe* (soft and sweet). It will introduce you to open and closed positions—you can read the section on open and closed positions on page 12 if you need to. Keep in mind that the positions should be held and not "built." In other words, the first and third string positions should be held together—don't place one finger on the third string and then the other on the first.

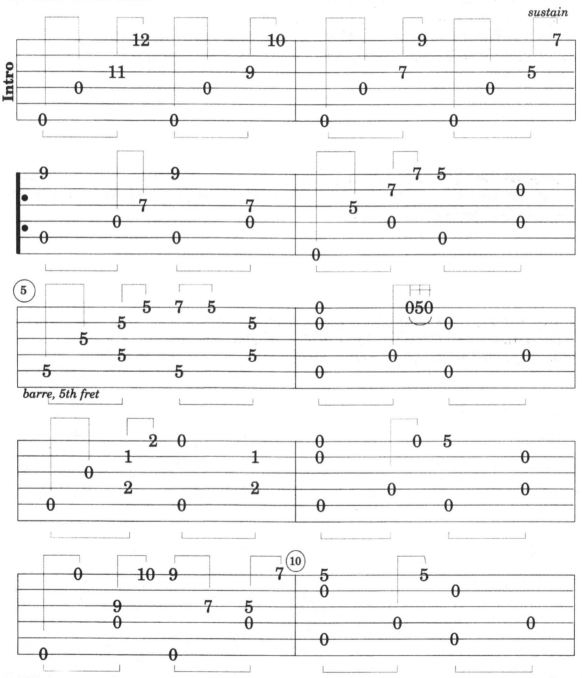

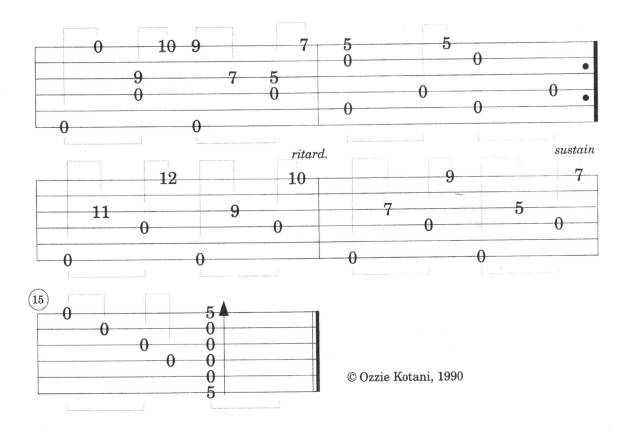

ritard.   *sustain*

(15)

© Ozzie Kotani, 1990

measures 1—2: A series of closed and open positions form the introduction to this piece. Play it slowly and regularly.

Use your pointer finger on the 3rd string and your little or ring finger on the 1st string. The 3rd and 1st string

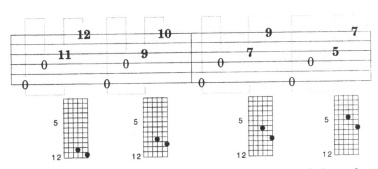

position should be held together. Don't place one finger on the 3rd string and then the other on the first.

Notice that the thumb of your right hand plays 6th and 4th strings only.

measure 3: The open position on frets 7 and 9 is held throughout. There should only be movement in the picking hand. Use your pointer finger on the 3rd string and your little or ring finger on the 1st string.

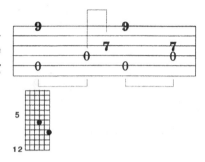

measure 4: The first half of this measure uses the open position on frets 5 and 7 with the addition of the second string held on the 7th fret. Because the author uses pointer and little fingers for open/closed positions, the ring finger is used to hold the 2nd string.

An option for players who use pointer and ring fingers for open/closed positions would be to use the ring finger to hold the 1st and 2nd strings on the 7th fret.

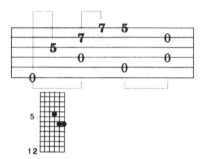

In the second half of the measure, drop the pointer from the 3rd string down to the first on the 5th fret or slide the finger holding the 1st string on the 7th fret down to the 5th.

measure 5: The word *barre* means that you hold down the guitar strings with one finger across several strings on the same fret. Some pointers:

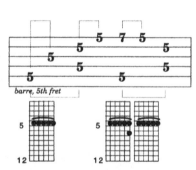

• The author places his pointer finger on the five strings to be plucked, excluding the 6th string. The middle finger comes over the pointer to add more pressure on the strings for a cleaner sound. Use the little finger to fret the first string on the 7th fret.

• If the sound is muffled or buzzing occurs, several factors may be involved. You should check your thumb position on the back of the guitar neck. It should be opposing the finger(s) on the 5th fret. Are you in the middle of the fret? See if getting closer to the fret bar improves the sound.

Try fretting all six strings. Experiment with placing your middle finger down first.

Finally, it may be that you need to develop finger strength or lower the action of your guitar. You could also use nylon strings or light gauge steel strings.

• Don't get frustrated if you can't get it right away. Be assured that your sound will improve over time. Never practice the barre to the point that your hand hurts or cramps up. Keep in mind that you only barre for one measure in most slack-key compositions. Anticipate and focus for that measure.

measure 6: Introduces a pinch that involves three strings. Your thumb plucks the 5th string, leaving you with three options for plucking the first and second strings:

• If you are playing a 2-finger style, brush upward with your pointer to strike both strings.

• If you are playing in a 3-finger style, use your pointer on the second string and middle finger on the first string.

• With a 4-finger style, like the author's, use the middle finger on the second string and the ring finger on the first string.

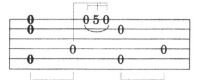

Play the hammer on the first string, 5th fret with the middle finger.

measure 7: Use the C chord position as follows: hold the 1st string, 2nd fret with your ring finger; the 2nd string, 1st fret with your pointer; and the fourth string 2nd fret with your middle finger.

Lift your ring finger to play the open first string; otherwise, hold the chord position throughout the measure.

Have your fingers in position **before** you pluck the strings. Again, don't build the chord a string at a time.

measure 9 & 11: Go back to the closed and open positions. Grab the 1st and 3rd strings in one movement, rather than building the positions. Use your pointer finger on the 3rd string and your little or ring finger on the 1st string.

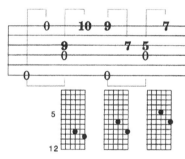

measures 13—14: Like the introduction. The same open and closed positions are used but the thumb and fingers of the right hand now alternate. Again, use your pointer finger on the 3rd string and your little or ring finger on the 1st string.

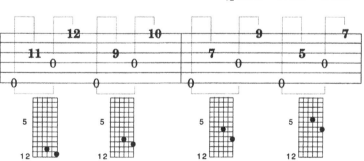

Play the measures slower and slower until the final open position. Hold it and let the notes sustain for a few beats. Then play the final measure with a strum across the final chord.

Exercise 4
ʻĀwīwī
Taro Patch—DGDGBD

This piece was taken from an exercise the author learned from his friend and first teacher, Peter Medeiros. Here, you are introduced to some faster playing. Start slowly and allow the bass to set the meter. After becoming familiar with the tune and the fingerings, try working up to your fastest pace without losing your timing. Challenge yourself but have fun doing it! ʻĀwīwī means "to hurry—quick and fast."

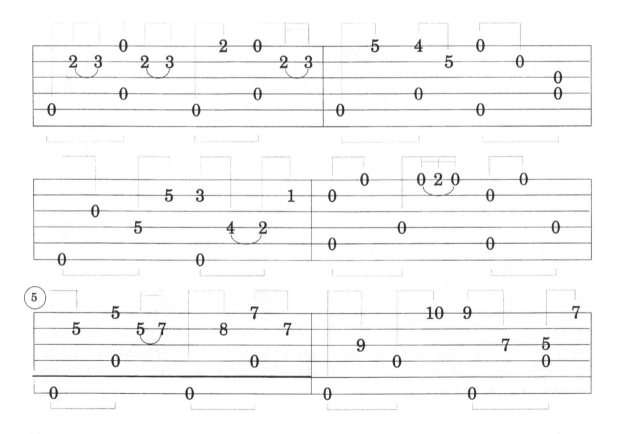

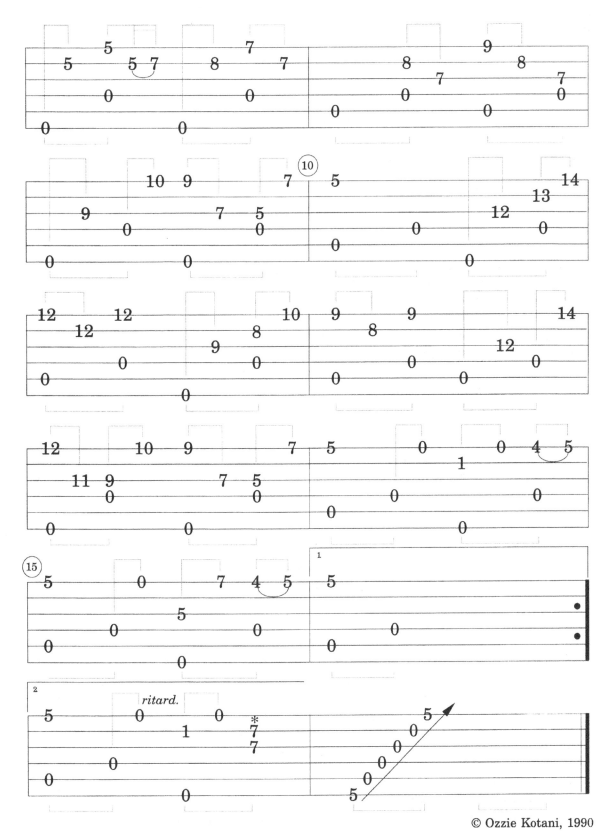

measure 1: Use your middle finger for the slides on the 2nd string. Use your pointer to add the note on the 1st string, 2nd fret.

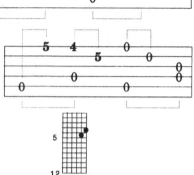

measure 2: Use your middle finger to hold the 1st string, 5th fret. Your pointer finger then holds the note on the 1st string 4th fret while your middle finger moves over to the 2nd string, 5th fret.

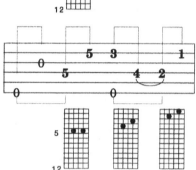

measure 3, left hand: Use your middle finger on the 4th string, 5th fret and your ring finger on the 2nd string, 5th fret. Your pointer then moves to the 2nd string, 3rd fret while your middle finger moves down to the 4th string, 4rd fret. The middle finger then slides down to the 4th string, 2nd fret and the pointer moves to the 2nd string, 1st fret. Using these particular fingers should keep them from getting tangled!

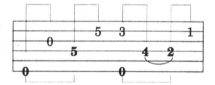

measure 3, right hand: The thumb plays the highlighted notes, including the slide on the 4th string from the 4th to the 2nd fret.

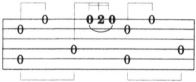

measure 4: See page ten for an explanation of hammers. Use your middle finger on the 1st string, 2nd fret.

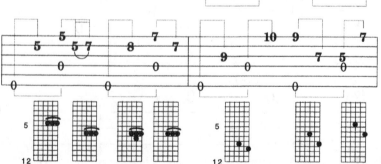

measures 5—6: To anticipate the open and closed positions in measure 6, use your pointer to hold down the 1st, 2nd and 3rd strings on the 5th fret. Quickly slide up to the 7th fret and use your middle finger to add the note on the 2nd string, 8th fret. You are now set up to use your pointer finger on the 3rd string and your little finger on the 1st string for the positions in measure 6.

measures 7—8: Measure 7 repeats measure 5. In measure 8, your pointer finger stays on the 1st, 2nd and 3rd strings, 7th fret while your middle finger holds the 2nd string, 8th fret and your little or ring finger holds the 1st string, 9th fret.

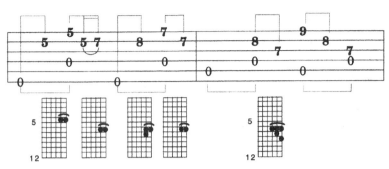

measures 9—10: A series of closed and open positions. Use your pointer finger on the 3rd string and your little or ring finger on the 1st string. End with your pointer finger on the 1st string, 5th fret at the beginning of measure 10.

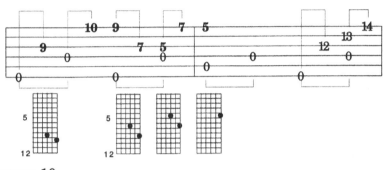

measures 10—11: Use your pointer finger across strings 1, 2 and 3 at the 12th fret. Add your middle finger on the 2nd string 13th fret and your ring finger on the 1st string, 14th fret. Then, at

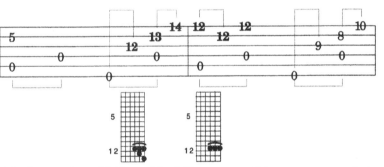

the beginning of measure 11, just take off the added fingers and leave your pointer alone across the 12th fret.

If you play a classical guitar with only twelve frets below the body, use your pointer finger on the 3rd string, rather than barring the three strings on the first chord.

measures 11—12: There are two ways to hold the position in the second half of measure 11. You can use your pointer finger on the 2nd string, 8th fret; your middle finger on the 3rd string, 9th fret; and your

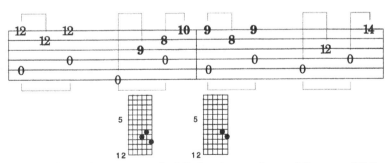

ring finger on the 1st string, 10th fret. Or you can hold the 1st string with your little finger which the author does.

measures 12—13: The tablature may look a little confusing here but it is not as hard as it looks. Notice that all you are doing is moving a series of open and closed positions down the neck. This is a classic slack key pattern and learning

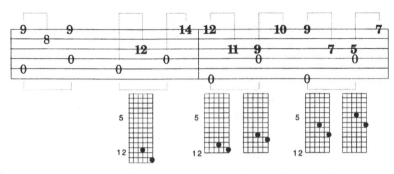

to play it smoothly will help you in with other tunes. Use your pointer finger on the 3rd string and your little or ring finger on the 1st string.

measures 14—15: In measure 14, use your pointer on the 2nd string, 1st fret and your ring or little finger for the slide on the 1st string from the 4th to the 5th fret. In measure 15, use your pointer finger

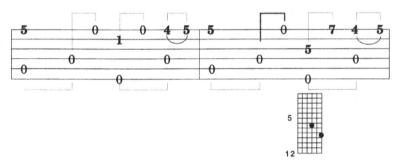

on the 3rd string, 5th fret and your little or ring finger on the 1st string, 7th fret. Then, use your pointer finger to hold the 1st string, 4th fret and add-on with your middle finger on the 5th fret.

measures 16—18: The repeat sign sends you back to the beginning of the piece. The second time through, skip measure 16 and play measure 17 instead. Measure 17 ends with a plucked chime: see page 11 to review chiming.

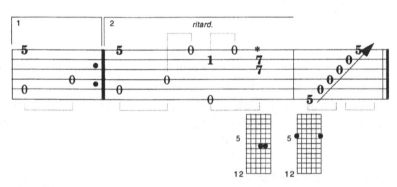

The plucked notes are played with the pointer and middle fingers of your right hand. Gradually slow your playing through this measure and let the chimes ring for a few beats. For the final strummed chord, the author uses his thumb to hold the 6th string, 5th fret and his ring finger to hold the 1st string, 5th fret.

Exercise 5
Maunaloa
Taro Patch—DGDGBD

This piece will take you through some variations on a fine old song that has been recorded by many slack key players. Written by Helen Parker, *Maunaloa* is about an interisland ship that sailed in the old days and was named after the "Long Mountain" on the Big Island.

This version will use all of the techniques you have learned so far.

Photo: Party group, post-1900. Courtesy of Bishop Museum Archives.

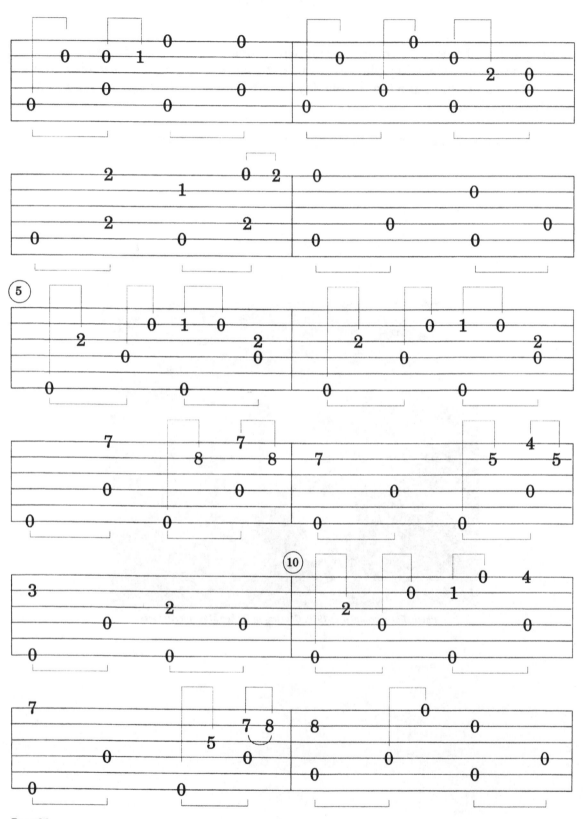

barre, 5th fret

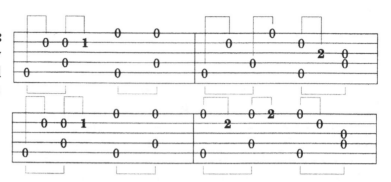

measures 1—2 & 15—16:
Use your pointer finger only
on the 2nd string, 1st fret and
your middle finger on the 1st
and 3rd strings, 2nd fret.

measure 3: Use the C chord position as follows: hold
the 1st string, 2nd fret with your ring finger; the 2nd
string, 1st fret with your pointer; and the fourth string
2nd fret with your middle finger. The only movement
comes when you lift your ring finger from the first string
and place it back on the fret.

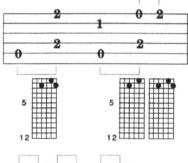

measures 5—6, 21—22 & 35: Use your middle finger
on the 3rd string, 2nd fret; and your pointer on the 2nd
string, 1st fret.

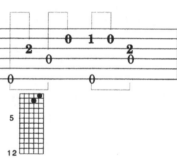

**measures 7—8, 23—24 &
37—38:** Use your pointer
finger on the 1st string, 7th
fret; and your middle finger
on the 2nd string, 8th fret.
This gets you ready for
measure 8: on the 2nd string,
move your middle finger

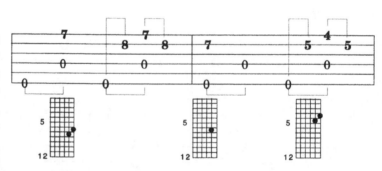

down from the 8th to the 7th fret, and then down again to the 5th fret. Your pointer
finger again holds the 1st string, now on the 4th fret.

measures 9, 25 & 39: After moving down to the 2nd
string, 3rd fret, the middle finger jumps to the 3rd
string, 2nd fret. Now you are ready for the following
measure.

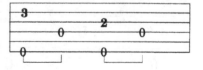

measure 10 & 26: As in measure 5, use your middle finger on the 3rd string, 2nd fret; your pointer on the 2nd string, 1st fret; and your little or ring finger on the 1st string, 4th fret.

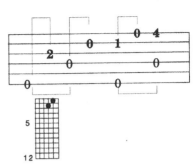

measures 11—12, 27—28 & 41—42: Continue up the 1st string to the 7th fret with your little finger. (If this feels uncomfortable, you may want to use your pointer finger for the slide in the previous measure and then hold the 7th fret position with either your ring or little finger.) Finally, add your pointer finger to the 3rd string, 5th fret. The author then uses his ring finger to slide from the 7th to the 8th fret on the 2nd string after releasing the 3rd string, 5th fret.

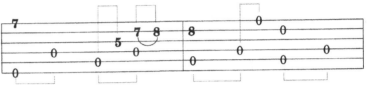

measures 13 & 29: A variation of the vamp in measures 5 and 10. Use your middle finger for the first string, 2nd fret; your pointer for the 2nd string, 1st fret; and your little finger for the slide from the 4th to the 5th fret on the 1st string.

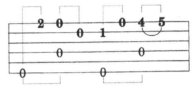

measures 14 & 30: A closed position: use your little or ring finger on the 1st string, 5th fret; and your pointer on the 3rd string, 4th fret. Be careful to let the open 2nd string ring without buzzing.

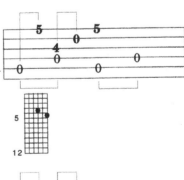

measures 17 & 33: Use your pointer for the barre across the 5th fret. Use your middle finger on top of the pointer to add more pressure to the barre. Use your little finger to add the note on the 2nd string, 7th fret.

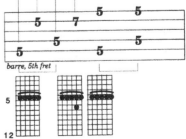

measures 18—19: Use your pointer finger on the 1st string, 9th fret and your middle finger on the 2nd string, 10th fret. After measure 18, bring your middle finger down from the 10th fret to the 8th fret on the

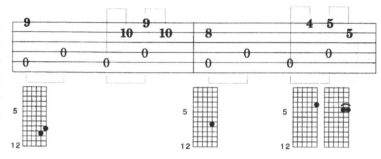

2nd string. Use your pointer finger to hold the 1st string, 4th fret and then your middle finger on both the first and second strings, 5th fret.

measures 31 & 32: Use your pointer finger on the 3rd string, 4th fret; and your middle finger on the 3rd string, 5th fret. Look at page 11 to review playing the two chime notes. The author uses his middle finger to play both notes on the 2nd and 3rd strings above the 12th fret.

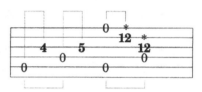

measure 34: Look at page 10 if you need to review the section on hammers. Use your middle finger on the 1st string, 5th fret.

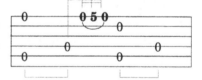

measure 36: Use your middle finger to the slide from the 2nd to the 3rd fret on the second string. The slide is played quickly, as if it were a single note. Then use your pointer finger to hold the 2nd string, 1st fret; and your middle finger to hold the 3rd string, 2nd fret.

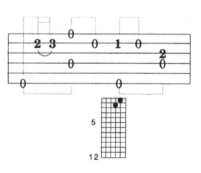

measure 40: A variation of measure 36. Use your little or ring finger on the 1st string, 4th fret.

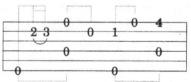

measures 44, 46 & 48: These are all open position chords. Use your pointer finger on the 3rd string and your little or ring finger on the 1st string. The example is from measure 44.

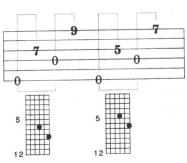

measures 45 & 47: For the closed position at the end of the measures, use your pointer finger on the 3rd string and your little or ring finger on the 1st string. The example is measure 45.

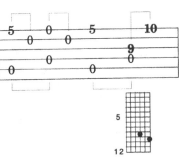

measure 49: Each note is sounded individually. Use your middle finger on the 6th string, 5th fret; your pointer finger on the 5th string, 4th fret; and your ring or little finger on the 1st string, 5th fret. Let the chord ring a bit before going on to the next measure:

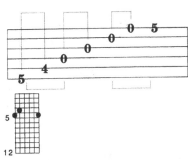

measure 50: The last measure is a slowly strummed chord. The author holds the 6th string, 5th fret with his middle finger, and the 1st string, 5th fret with his ring finger.

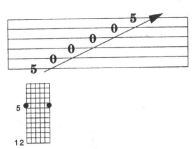

Exercise 6
Manamana Lele
Taro Patch—DGDGBD

The translation of "Manamana Lele" is "Jumping Fingers." With all the hammers in the piece, your fingers will be jumping!

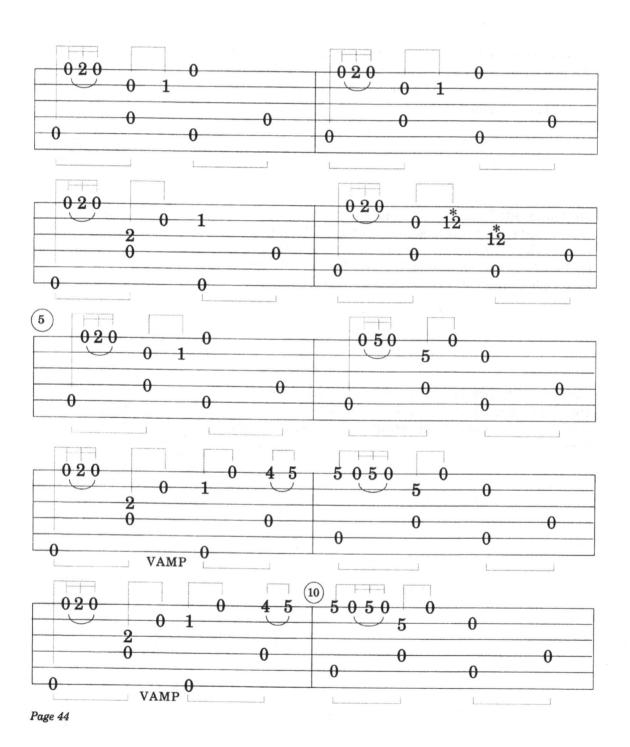

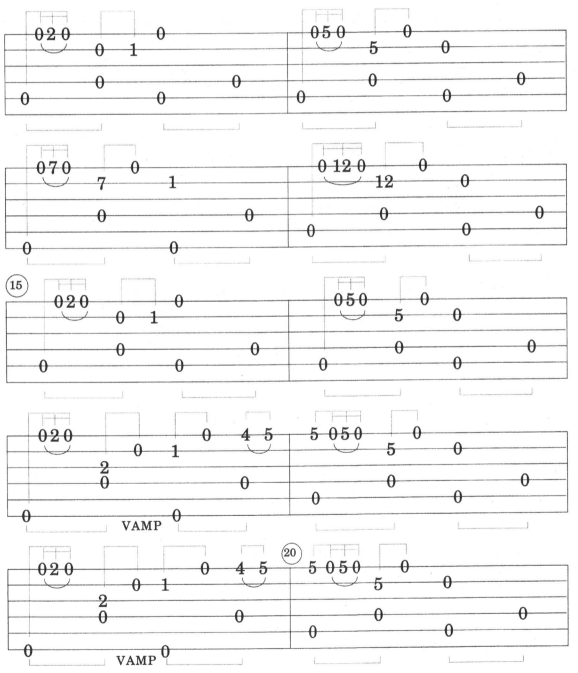

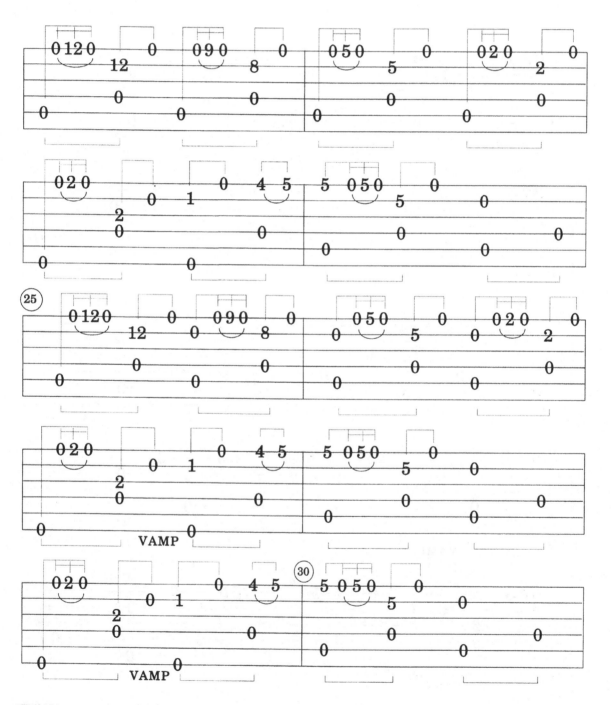

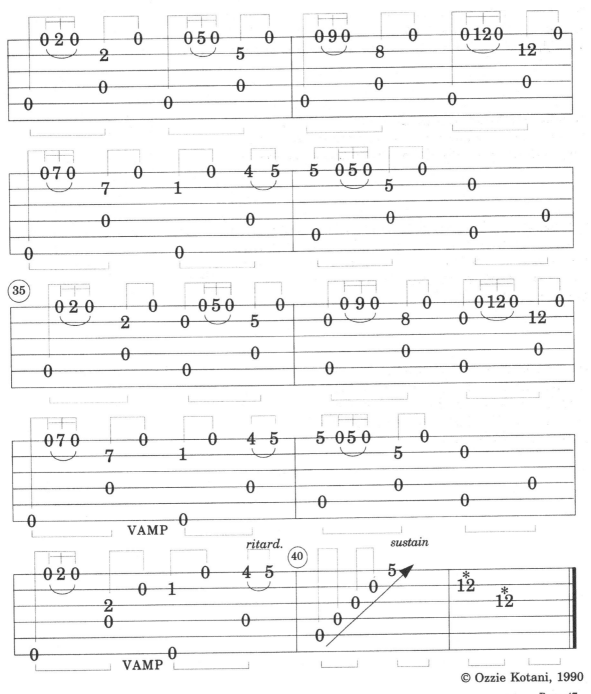

The author uses the following fingers in this exercise: the pointer finger holds the second string on the first fret only; the middle finger holds down all other frets on the 2nd string.

measure 1: Look at the paragraph on page 10 about hammers. The whole piece is made up of hammers and measure 1 is a typical example. The author uses his middle finger to do the hammer on the 1st string, 2nd fret. Then the pointer finger holds the note on the 2nd string, 1st fret.

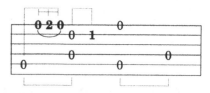

measure 4: Look at page 11 to review playing the two chime notes. The author uses his middle finger to play both notes on the 2nd and 3rd strings above the 12th fret.

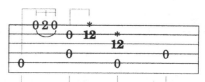

measure 7 & 9: After the hammer, use your middle finger to hold the 3rd string, 2nd fret; your pointer finger to hold the 2nd string, 1st fret; and your little finger again to hold the slide on the 1st string from the 4th to the 5th fret.

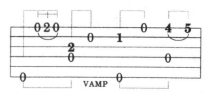

measures 40—41: Slowly play the chord so that each note sounds individually. Pause and then play the two chimed notes with your middle fingers on the 2nd and 3rd strings above the 12th fret.

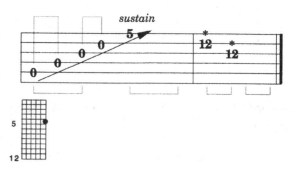

SLACK G OR DOUBLE SLACK TUNING
D G D F# B D

The next tuning gets its name because the guitar is slacked to open G (Taro Patch) and then the third string (G) is slacked further down to F#.

The late Auntie Alice Namakelua was known for playing in this tuning and it has been called Namakelua's tuning as well.

Slack key masters Sonny Chillingworth and Raymond Kane have recorded beautiful compositions in this tuning. Sonny's famous virtuoso piece, "Whee Ha Swing," reveals his inventive and creative genius in using a tuning that many guitarists find limited.

Follow the procedures for getting into the Taro Patch Tuning, then lower your third string **half a step to F#**. Check your tuning by following the method outlined under the Taro Patch Tuning section on page 17. Hold the following frets:

6 5 4 3 2 1
5 7 4 5 3

Note that holding the third string down on the first fret brings you back up to G and that you can strum a full G chord after doing so. This position—pointer on the third string, first fret— is referred to as "home base" in the sense that you always return to it or hold it often when playing in this tuning. Not covering this position allows the lowered third string to ring out if touched and creates unpleasant dissonance in the sound.

I am sure you will enjoy the exercise in this tuning. It is the first step towards playing in a "closed" tuning which requires you to hold a position. It also introduces you to a new bass pattern.

Exercise 7
‘Ewalu
Slack G (Double Slack)—DGDF#BD

Photo: ‘Ukulele factory, no date. Courtesy of Bishop Museum Archives.

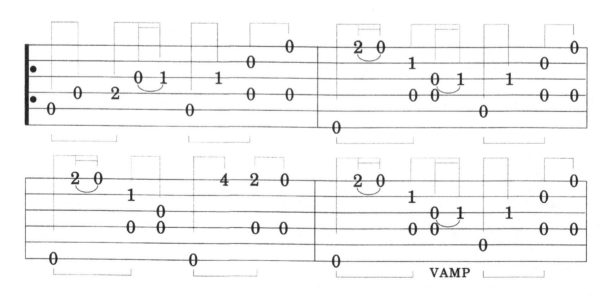

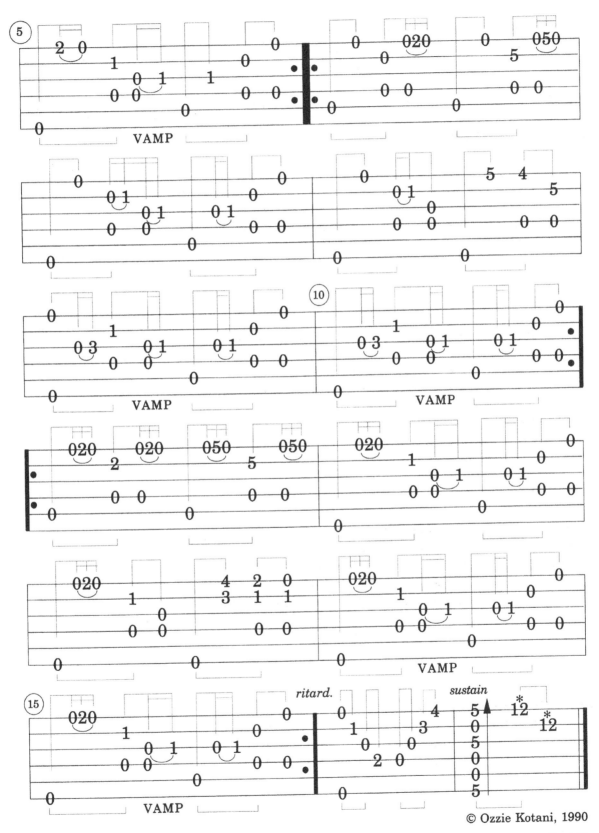

This piece introduces you to a new bass pattern. The thumb plays the 5th and 4th strings (as shown) or the 6th and 4th strings. Listen carefully to the tape to get the pattern. The author refers to the repeated 4th string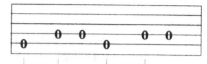

bass as a "pinch, pinch" movement, because, in this composition, the 4th string bass is always played along with another string. Tie measures 1 and 2 together and play them several times to get a feel for the pattern.

measure 1: This measure has the exception to the right hand thumb pattern. Here, the thumb plays the first three notes.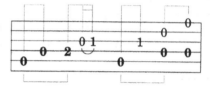

Use the middle finger to hold the 4th string, 2nd fret; then, use the pointer finger on the 3rd string, 1st fret— and **leave it on for the rest of the measure**. You are no longer in an open tuning. Your pointer finger on the 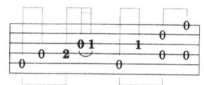 3rd string, 1st fret is "home base" in the tuning and failure to hold this position allows the slackened 3rd string to ring out.

measure 2: Use your middle finger to pull-off from the 1st string, 2nd fret to the open 1st string. Then fret the 2nd string, 1st fret with your pointer finger. Your pointer is also used to play the add-on on the 3rd string 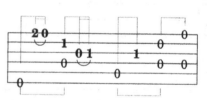 1st fret and to hold that position at the end of the measure.

measure 3: After pulling-off with your middle finger and fretting the 2nd string with the pointer, as in measure 2, use your ring finger to fret the 1st string, 4th fret followed by your pointer finger on the 1st string, 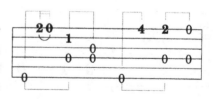 2nd fret.

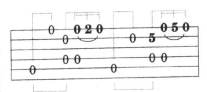

measure 6: In this measure you will be "pinching" while hammering: immediately after pinching the open 4th and 1st strings, hammer the 1st string on the indicated fret. Use your middle finger for hammering and to fret the 2nd string.

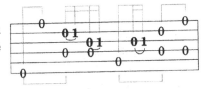

measure 7: Use your pointer finger to play the add-on on the 2nd string, 1st fret and your pointer finger for the add-on on the 3rd string, 1st fret.

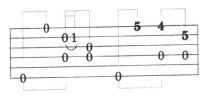

measure 8: For the second half of the measure, the author uses his middle finger to fret the 1st string, 5th fret; his pointer finger on the 1st string, 4th fret; and his middle finger again on the 2nd string, 5th fret.

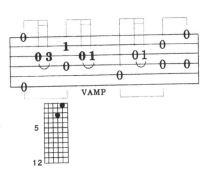

measures 9 & 10: Try using your ring finger for the add-on on the 3rd string, 3rd fret and your pointer finger on the 2nd string, 1st fret. The author frets both strings at the same time when executing this add-on to "anticipate" the next fretted note and to minimize left hand movement. Use your pointer finger for the rest of the measure.

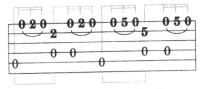

measure 11: The pinched hammering sequences in the following measures create a dynamic and dramatic presentation for this last section of the piece. You can use your middle finger to hammer on the 1st string and to fret the 2nd string; then return to hammer the 1st string with your middle finger again. This pattern is used by slack key master Sonny Chillingworth.

measure 12: Use your middle finger to hammer on the first string, 2nd fret and your pointer to fret the 2nd string, 1st fret. The use your pointer again for the add-ons on the 3rd string, 1st fret.

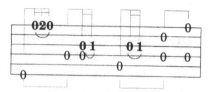

measure 13: After hammering with your middle finger and fretting with your pointer, **slide** your pointer up to the 2nd string, 3rd fret and bring your ring finger down on the 1st string, 4th fret. Then slide this position down two frets to the 2nd string, 1st fret and the 1st string 2nd fret. Finally, lift your ring finger off the 1st string for the last pinch.

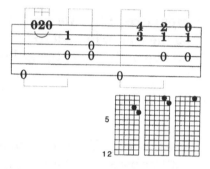

measure 16: For the first half of the measure, use your pointer finger to hold the 2nd string, 1st fret while your middle finger holds the 4th string, 2nd fret. After plucking the 4th string, 2nd fret and while you are playing the next two open strings, lift your middle finger off and begin sliding your pointer up to the 2nd string, 3rd fret. Then use your ring finger to fret the 1st string, 4th fret.

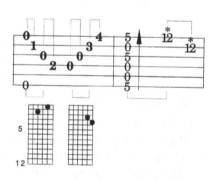

For the final chord, use your ring finger on the 1st string, 5th fret, your middle finger on the 3rd string, 5th fret and your thumb on the 6th string, 5th fret. The strum across the strings is quick and strong. Look at page 11 to review playing the two chime notes. The author uses his middle finger to play both notes on the 2nd and 3rd strings above the 12th fret.

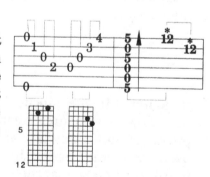

Exercise 8
Kakahiaka
Slack G (Double Slack)—DGDF#BD

"Kakahiaka" means "morning" in Hawaiian and this short instrumental starts like the ticking of a clock but wakes up in a hurry!

Photo by Alfred Mitchell: Guitar players, Puna, Hawai'i, 1892. Courtesy of Bishop Museum Archives.

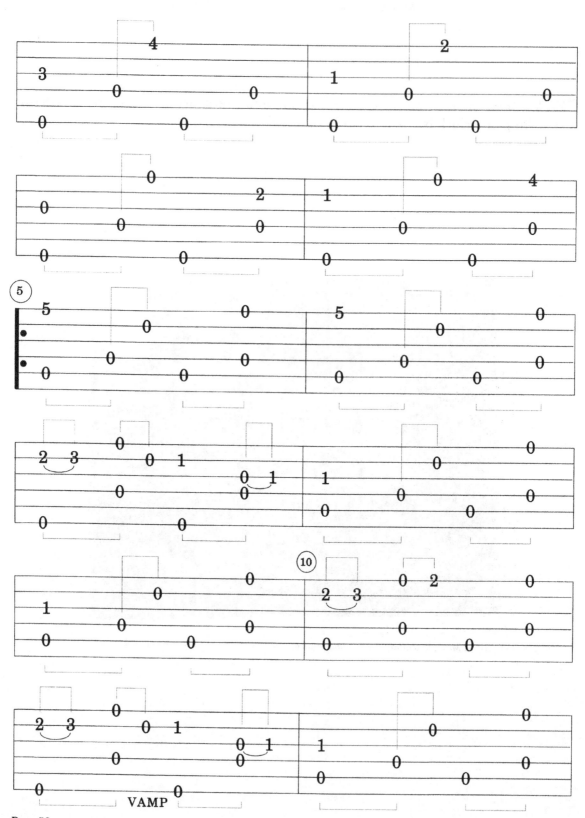

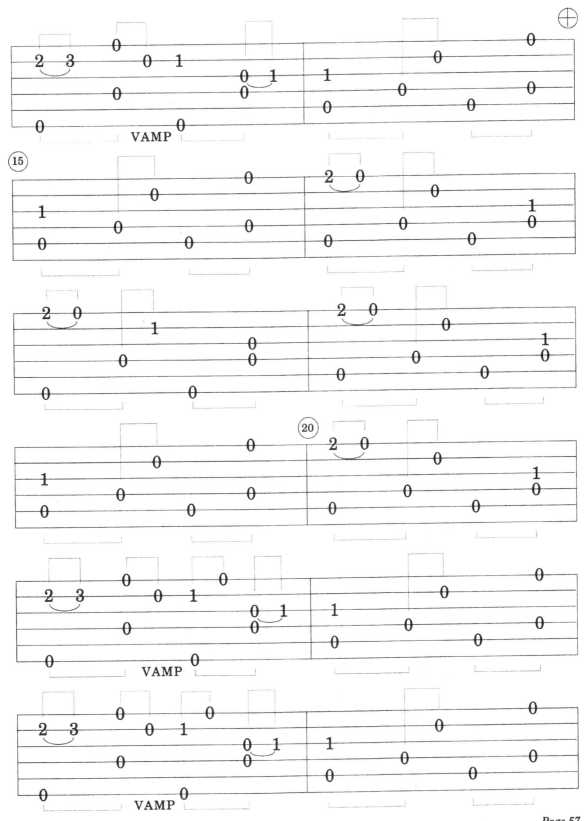

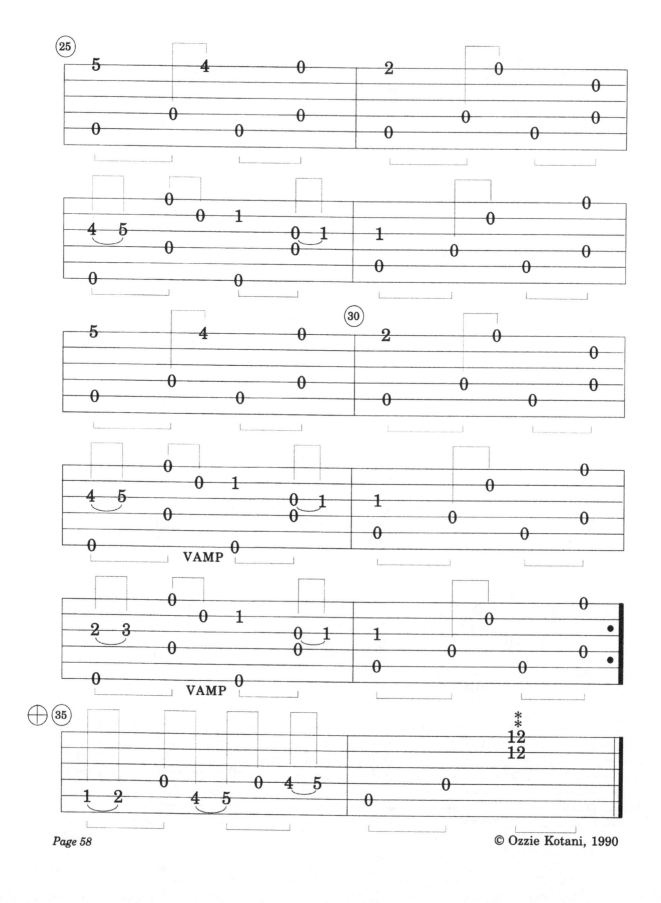

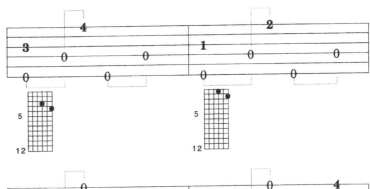

measures 1—2: To hold these two closed positions, use your pointer finger on the 3rd string and your little or ring finger on the 1st string.

measures 3—4: Use your pointer or middle finger on the 2nd string, 2nd fret in measure 3. Then, use your pointer finger on the 2nd string, 1st fret in measure 4. The author reaches up to the 1st string, 4th fret with his little finger to minimize hand movement.

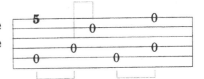

measures 5 & 6: Continuing from measure 4, your little finger moves to the 1st string, 5th fret. Use the same fingering in measure 6.

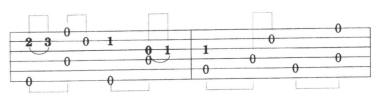

measures 7—8: The movement on the 2nd string, from the 2nd fret to the 3rd fret, can be played as an add-on or a slide. For the add-on, use your pointer finger on the 2nd fret and your middle finger on the 3rd fret. For the slide, use either your pointer or middle finger. This applies to all the following measures that have this movement.

Use your pointer to hold the 2nd string, 1st fret and for the add-on on the 3rd string, 1st fret. Just keep the position throughout measure 8.

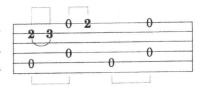

measure 10: This is similar to measure 7. Following the movement from the 2nd to the 3rd fret on the 2nd string, use your pointer finger to hold the 1st string, 2nd fret.

Exercise 8, Kakahiaka, page 5

measure 16: While your pointer finger holds the 3rd string, 1st fret, use your ring finger to pull-off on the 1st string, 2nd fret.

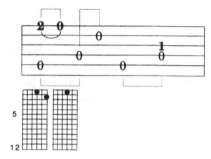

measure 17: Move your pointer finger to the 2nd string, 1st fret while your ring finger again does the pull-off on the 1st string, 2nd fret.

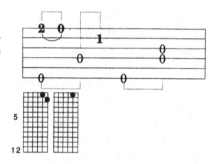

measure 18: After the pull-off, your pointer finger now returns to "home base" on the 3rd string, 1st fret for a repeat of what was done in measure 16.

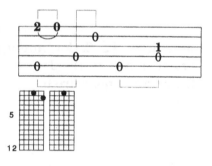

measure 25: The author uses his middle finger on the 1st string, 5th fret and then his pointer finger on the 1st string, 4th fret.

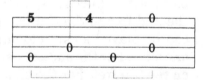

measure 26: Use your pointer or middle finger to hold the 1st string, 2nd fret.

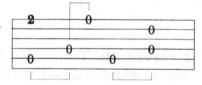

measures 27—28 & 31—32: For the add-on on the 3rd string, the author uses his pointer finger on the 4th fret

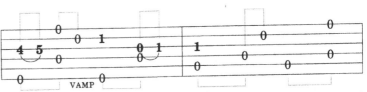

and his middle finger on the 5th fret. Then, use your pointer finger to hold the 2nd string, 1st fret and to play the add-on on the 3rd string, 1st fret.

measures 33—34: Note that the movement from the 2nd fret to the 3rd fret is on the 3rd string in this

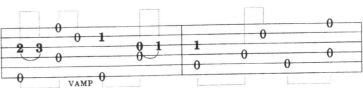

measure. Follow the same fingering suggestions given for measure 7.

measure 34: The repeat sign sends you back to measure 5 to begin the piece again. Play to the end of measure 14 where you will see a coda (⊕) sign. After playing this measure, skip down to measure 35, to the second coda, and end the piece.

measure 35: For this final bass run that ends the piece, use your right hand thumb to play the add-ons on the 5th and 4th strings. Your right hand pointer finger or thumb will pluck the open 4th string both times.

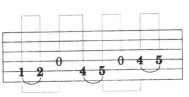

Your left hand pointer holds the 5th string, 1st fret and your middle frets the add-on on the 2nd fret; use the same combination for the add-on on the 5th string from the 4th to the 5th fret; and again for the 4th string from the 4th to the 5th fret.

measure 36: Your right hand thumb plays the open 5th and 4th strings. Depending on your picking style, use your right hand pointer and middle fingers or your middle and ring fingers to pluck the 12th fret chimes on the 1st and 2nd strings.

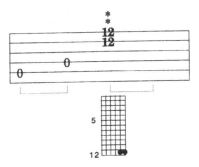

DROP C TUNING
C G D G B D

This tuning is the second major branch off from the Open G or Taro Patch tuning. Unlike the Slack G tuning, it changes the key from G to C.

Follow the procedures for getting into the Taro Patch tuning, then "drop," or lower, the sixth string **a whole step to C.** Check this note by holding down the second string on the first fret. Check your tuning by by following the method outlined under the Taro Patch Tuning section on page 17. Hold the following frets:

                6 5 4 3 2 1
                7 7 5 4 3

"Home base" in this "closed" tuning is: your pointer on the 2nd string, 1st fret; your middle finger on the 4th string, 2nd fret; and your ring finger on the 1st string, 2nd fret. Strumming this position should give you a full C chord. As in the Slack G tuning, you will always come back to the "home base" position when playing in this tuning.

Photo: Three female musicians. Courtesy of Bishop Museum Archives.

Exercise 9
Namaka's Mele
Drop C—CGDGBD

"Namaka's Mele" was composed by the author for Kumu Hula Patience Namaka Bacon. Her calm, quiet, and sometimes mischievous nature has endeared her to many. With all due respect, this one's for Pat.

Photo: Four hula dancers with guitarist, pre-1900. Courtesy of Bishop Museum Archives.

Exercise 9, Namaka's Mele, page 1

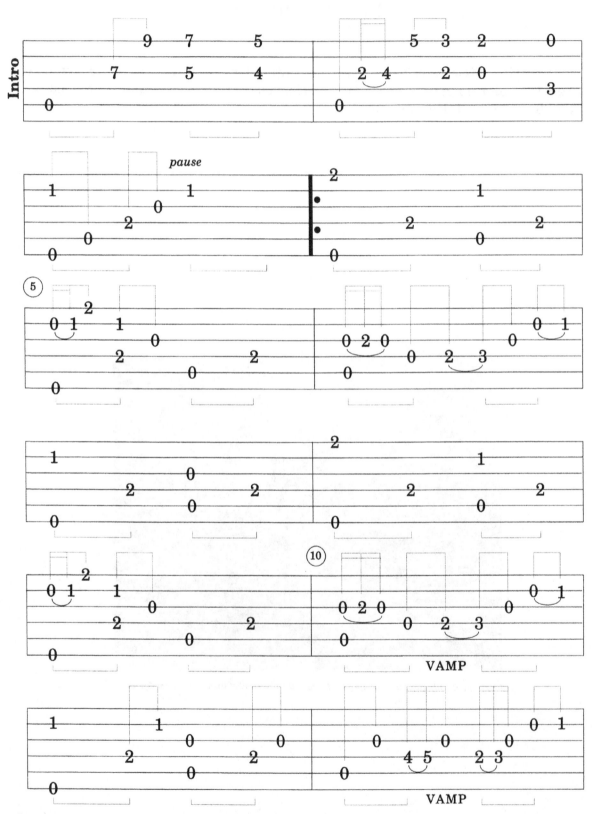

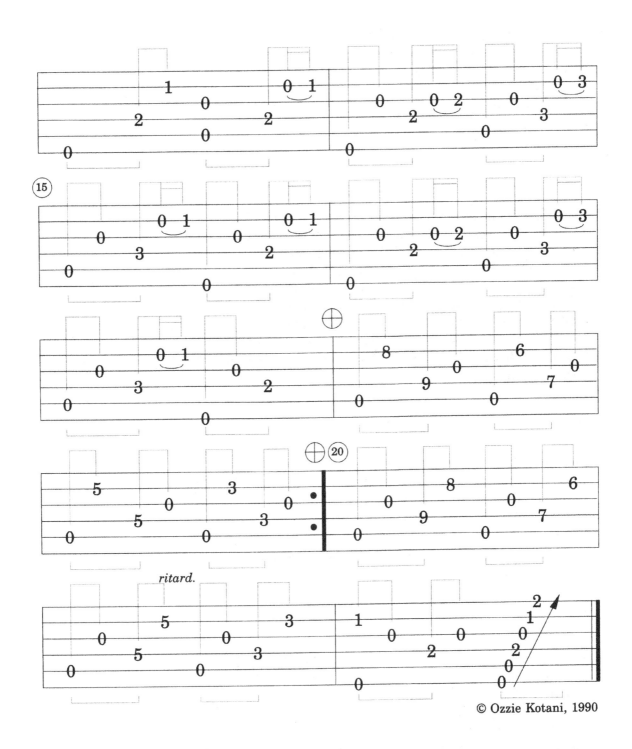

measure 1: The introduction begins with a sequence of open and closed positions on the 1st and 3rd strings. You will notice that there is no steady meter in this section if you listen carefully to the cassette tape.

Use your pointer finger on the 3rd string and your little or ring finger on the 1st string.

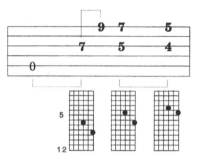

measure 2: The slide on the 3rd string from the 2nd to the 4th fret leads into a closed position. Use your pointer for the 3rd string slide and then add your little or ring finger to the 1st string, 5th fret. Next, using the same fingers, move the closed position down two frets to the 3rd string, 2nd fret and the 1st string, 3rd fret. Then, drop your pointer finger down to the 1st string, 2nd fret. Finally, use your middle finger to hold the 4th string, 3rd fret. You are now in position to hold "home base" in the following measure.

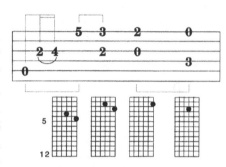

measure 3: Use your pointer on the 2nd string, 1st fret; your middle finger on the 4th string, 2nd fret; and your ring finger on the 1st string, 2nd fret to hold the home base C chord. Although you will not pluck the 1st string in this measure, hold the full chord. Pause for a beat or two before beginning the next section.

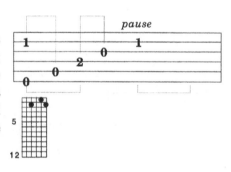

measure 4: Holding the C chord, we begin the metered section from this measure. **Your right hand thumb should still be used on the 6th, 5th, and 4th strings** in this tuning. Note that the bass pattern will be alternating in a different sequence when you are holding home base. In reference to the strings, you will be plucking a 6-4-5-4 bass pattern as opposed to the more common 5-4-5-4-6-4-6-4 pattern used in the Taro Patch and Slack G tunings.

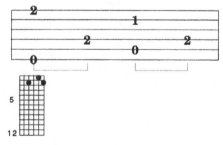

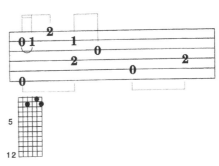

measure 5: While holding home base, use your pointer finger to play the add-on on the 2nd string, 1st fret. Although you may not "see" the chord in the second half of the measure, hold the home base position throughout the measure. This will minimize hand movement and develop a feel for holding the key position in this tuning.

measure 6: Begins with a pinch on the open 5th and 3rd strings. After the pinch, use your middle finger to add-on and pull-off on the 3rd string, 2nd fret to create a "slow" hammer. You can use your middle finger to slide on the 4th string from the 2nd to the 3rd fret; or you can use your pointer finger on the 4th string, 2nd fret and your middle finger to add-on on the 3rd fret. You can also use your middle and ring fingers in place of your pointer and middle fingers.

The final add-on brings you back to home base, so use your pointer on the 2nd string, 1st fret and build your full chord for the following two measures.

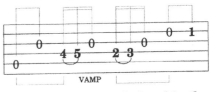

measure 12: Left hand: use your pointer and middle finger combination for the add-ons on the 4th string. This gives you better control and a clearer sound than sliding. Again, use your pointer on the 2nd string, 1st fret at then end of the measure to anticipate holding the C chord in the following measure.

Right hand: your thumb plays the notes on the 5th and 4th strings.

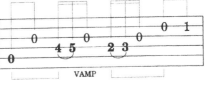

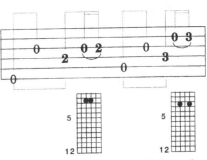

measures 14 & 16: Use your pointer finger to add-on on the 3rd string, 2nd fret. At the same time, move your middle finger from the 4th string, 2nd fret to the 4th string, 3rd fret. Use your ring finger again for the add-on on the 2nd string, 3rd fret.

You will use the same position for the first part of the next measure. A key to smoother playing is to minimize your left hand movement. Anticipating what will happen in the following measure will help tremendously in making the playing of slack key easier for you. By leaving your middle finger as an anchor on the 4th string, your playing will be smooth and you will be ready for the following measure.

measures 15 & 17: Keep your middle finger on the 3rd string, 3rd and 2nd frets and play the add-on with your pointer finger on the 2nd string, 1st fret. The second add-on in the middle of the measure brings you back to the C chord home base.

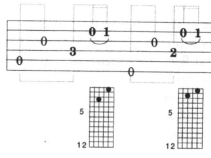

measure 18—19: A progression of positions coming down on the 4th and 2nd strings. Like the open and closed positions, these should be held and not built as you pluck the strings.

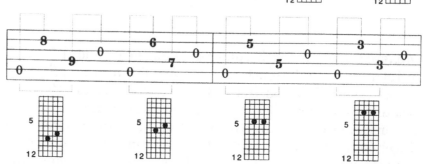

Start with your middle finger on the 4th string, 9th fret and your pointer finger on the 2nd string, 8th fret. These same fingers move down to the 7th and 6th frets for the second half of the measure.

In measure 19, leave your middle finger on the 4th string, 5th fret but replace your pointer with your ring finger on the 2nd string, 5th fret. These same fingers then move down to the 3rd fret on both strings for the second half of the measure.

measure 19: At the end of the measure there is a repeat sign and a coda (⊕) sign. The repeat sends you back to measure 4. Play through to measure 17 where there is another coda sign. After you play measure 17, jump over to measure 20.

measures 20—21: The same positions you held in measures 18—19 are held in these two measures, but the picking pattern has changed. Your right hand

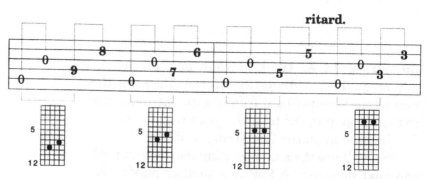

thumb and fingers still alternate. Note the *ritard* in measure 21 as you approach the end of the piece.

measure 22: Hold home base throughout the measure and finish with a full, slow strum.

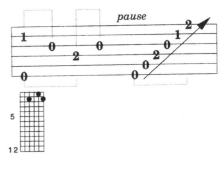

Made in the USA
Las Vegas, NV
08 August 2024

93548118R00044